The Occasionally Accurate Annals of Football

"I love Dan Patrick. I love his hair. I love his laugh. Heck, I love his musk . . . and now, I love his writing. No one is better equipped to blend humor with weird fun facts about the NFL than Dan Patrick. I repeat, no one. AND IF YOU DISAGREE I WILL FIGHT YOU!!"

—Will Ferrell

"If you're a football fan, you need to have this book. You can read about the historic, iconic moments, as well as the obscure 'who cares' moments. And it's done in a funny, enlightening way by one of my favorite people, Dan Patrick. It's the perfect gift for someone who loves the National Football League."

—Tony Dungy, former NFL defensive back and head coach

"Talk about your perfect match: One of the greatest sports media interviewers and storytellers of all time has written a book about the NFL, the greatest narrative generating machine in American sports history. This book is a treasure trove of exactly what you'd expect."

—Rich Eisen, sports broadcasting legend

"Dan Patrick is a TV star, radio raconteur, now author—he's the Jim Thorpe of media members—known for his versatility and longevity. Only Dan can tackle the NFL in this way—with his trademark irreverence, wit and institutional knowledge of the game—to produce this most entertaining and fun book, a must read for DP fans past, present and future."

—Andrea Kremer, Pro Football Hall of Fame journalist

"I never learned so much and at the same time absolutely nothing at all. I highly recommend this book to anyone who has empty shelf space that would look just a little bit better if it displayed a book carrying the name of one of America's broadcasting icons."

—Mike Florio, creator of ProFootballTalk

"Dan Patrick is a mentor, leader, and friend."

—Rodney Harrison

Also by Dan Patrick

The Big Show: Inside ESPN's Sportscenter (with Keith Olbermann)

Outtakes: Dan Patrick

Also by Joel H. Cohen

How to Lose a Marathon: A Starter's Guide to Finishing in 26.2 Chapters

THE OCCASIONALLY ACCURATE
ANNALS OF
FOOTBALL

The NFL's Greatest Players,
Plays, Scandals, and Screw-Ups

(Plus Stuff We Totally Made Up)

Dan Patrick and Joel H. Cohen

BenBella Books, Inc.
Dallas, TX

BenBella Books, Inc.
10440 N. Central Expressway
Suite 800
Dallas, TX 75231
benbellabooks.com
Send feedback to feedback@benbellabooks.com

BenBella is a federally registered trademark.

Printed in the United States of America
10 9 8 7 6 5 4 3 2 1

Library of Congress Control Number: 2023003652
ISBN 9781637743683 (print)
ISBN 9781637743690 (ebook)

Editing by Alyn Wallace and Leah Wilson
Copyediting by Elizabeth Degenhard
Proofreading by Ashley Casteel and Michael Fedison
Indexing by WordCo Indexing Services
Text design by Faceout Studio, Paul Nielsen
Text composition by Aaron Edmiston
Images on pages xiv, 8, 10, and 179 from the the public domain
Image on page 42 by RC Designs
Helmet illustrations by Codey Dauch Art
Other illustrations by Brian Bowens
Cover design by Brigid Pearson
Cover image © Shutterstock / MG SG (football); © Shutterstock / Jazmine Thomas (grass)
Printed by Versa Press

Special discounts for bulk sales are available. Please contact bulkorders@benbellabooks.com.

For my wife, Susan
(assuming she's okay being associated with this)

DAN

For my wife and family
(who have already told me they are not okay being associated with this)

JOEL

CONTENTS

I asked Adam Sandler to write a foreword for this book and he said yes. I was thrilled. This is, after all, ADAM SANDLER— movie star, TV star, recipient of the Mark Twain Prize for American Humor, and three-time Grammy Award nominee (if he had won, I would have said "winner").

There was only one problem—neither of us really knew what a foreword should look like. Instead of asking someone or making any efforts to figure it out, I told him, "Just write about football." He did, and here it is. Please consider this to be a foreword, whatever the hell that is.

—Dan

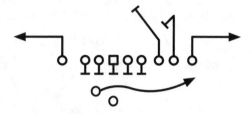

FOREWORD

Hi, my name is Adam Sandler, and I am a Jets fan.

When I was a kid, I was a Jets fan. And a Giants fan. And even a Bills fan. Anything New York because that's where I was from. That gave me a lot of good teams to choose from and a lot of stars to love. I actually think I was a Raiders fan too because they were known for being tough and dirty, and in my head I felt like that was a New York attitude, so I allowed myself to like them.

Joe Namath got us a Super Bowl when I was two years old. Every lady loved the man. I did, too. I also loved Emerson Boozer. I loved Don Maynard. I also thought Mike Battle was a badass. My brother got John Riggins's autograph a few years later at Jets camp. Riggins won Rookie of the Year that year. Everything was wonderful. New York was the coolest place on the planet, and I was proud to be a New Yorker.

Then my family moved to New Hampshire when I was five years old 'cause my dad got a job there. Off we went. My parents. My two sisters. My brother. And me. It was a great place, too. Lots of trees. Lots of lakes. Lots of fun. And lots of new friends. It was awesome there, and I loved it very much. But it got really cold in the winter. So one day I wore my wool hat to keep warm while walking to school. It was a green hat with a pom-pom on it. It also had the word "Jets" on the side. I got to the bottom of my street when I saw a bunch of other kids who were walking to the same school. "What's with that stupid hat?" I heard. *They couldn't be talking to me*, I thought. My grandmother bought me that hat, so I didn't like the sound of "stupid hat" when I knew my grandmother went out to a store, saw something, and thought I'd like it. "The Jets suck!" is what I heard next. That hurt. I think I actually teared up a little, but I didn't want anyone to see, 'cause I was five, new in town, and feeling new feelings. And that feeling was pride.

That night I discussed what went on with my family. My brother, Scott, said, "You live in New England now, of course you're going to hear the Jets suck. Everybody here are Patriots fans. Jim Plunkett fans. Sam 'Bam' Cunningham fans. Randy Vataha fans." I said, "So they don't hate Grandma?" My family all said, "No, they just hate the Jets." I said, "Do they hate the Giants and the Bills and the Raiders?" My dad said, "Probably, but they hate the Jets the most because they are in the same division as the Pats." That's the day I said, "Well, if they're gonna hate who I like, I might as well stick with the team they hate the most."

It was a lifetime decision that has given me a lot of humiliation and stomachaches, but I will never let go. At the beginning of every season, I hear a lot of doubt from people talking about my Jets. But I stare them down as if to say, "I know something you don't." (My best acting to date.)

Some seasons start off hot and cool off. Some seasons start off cold but get hot. Some seasons we make the playoffs. Most seasons we don't. But when we are rolling, it sure feels good. I know better than to ever get cocky—but when we get on a winning streak, or have incredible moments from incredible players? Man, it's worth the pain. Atkinson. Revis. Snell. Gastineau. Freeman McNeil. Wesley Walker. Klecko. Lyons. Toon. Mangold. Sanchez. Keyshawn. Chrebet. Love those guys for life. And so many others. The joy they could bring me was absolutely beyond.

And damn. So many great players on the team right now. Love you guys. I believe in you guys, 'cause I know you want it, too. Super Bowl rings and the chance for me to return to New Hampshire wearing that green pom-pom hat that Grandma bought me at Herman's Sporting Goods. And the ability to find that kid who was nasty to me so many years ago and say, "The Jets don't suck, buddy. You suck!"

Let's get it done, Jets.

Love,

Adam Sandler (Jets fan for life!)

Battledore and Shuttlecock.

1918—Hard to believe, but just two years later, this sport would transform into the NFL.

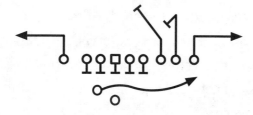

INTRODUCTION

"Baseball can suck it."
—Maya Angelou (we think)

Football, not baseball, is America's national sport. Baseball is merely "America's pastime," and pastimes are just that—things to pass time, like quilting or prison. Football is much more, a national obsession. In 2021, twenty-three of the twenty-five top-rated telecasts were NFL games! Football is so popular that games scheduled on the last Thursday in November even turn Thanksgiving into a national holiday.

It's no surprise the game's beloved. Football is fun, flashy, and entertaining—like Las Vegas the first hour you get there. It's also flawed, controversial, and dangerous—like Vegas the entire rest of your stay. Ultimately, though, the bad is forgotten in the spectacle of athleticism, entertainment, and those hats Green Bay fans wear that sort of look like cheese. (Cheese bras are also available if you're looking to buy a female fan a gift she'll probably hate.)

This book is a collection of reflections, thoughts, truths, lies, comments, and incredibly incorrect explanations and retellings of all things football. In it, you'll find contributions from fans who also happen to be writers from *The Simpsons, Modern Family, Saturday Night Live, The ESPY Awards, Late Night with Conan O'Brien*, and, thanks to a medium that talks to the dead, writers from both *Leave It to Beaver* and the Bible. We'll cover teams, players, plays, scandals, and more—and sometimes, also less! This is a collective love letter to football that also acknowledges its flaws. (By the way, in actual love letters it's better *not* to include the subject's flaws—voice of experience.)

The intent is to educate a little and entertain a lot. Comedy is meant to prevail over accuracy, but with our group's poor work ethic, some facts may accidentally slip in. Apologies in advance.

Dan and Joel

NOTE: There are a lot of players mentioned in this book. There are also some not mentioned. So, how did we choose? We included most of the top 100 players ever (as chosen by the NFL) and the "greats" from each team, and threw in others because they were famous, funny, or their moms ran into our moms and asked if they could be in the book. Even with those exacting methods, we missed some players, and, in doing so, hurt some feelings. If you are upset by some oversight in this book, we suggest you take all your anger, put it in a letter, and mail it to:

905 West Fulton Market, Suite 200
Chicago, IL 60607

NOTE: That's not our address. It's the company that makes Oreos. You probably won't get your complaint addressed, but you may get some free Oreos (and really, isn't that better?).

NOTE: This will be the last note in this book.

NOTE: No, it won't.

Do You Know What Footballs Are Made Of?

If you're guessing good wishes and rainbows, laced together with the eyelashes of naughty trolls, you're mostly wrong but clearly have a wonderful imagination (which you should really add to your LinkedIn profile!).

Footballs, commonly known as "pigskins," were actually never made from pigskin. The closest they got was when early footballs were made of pig bladders. That's right, pig bladders. A concept not attractive to players or the pigs.

As you might imagine (yes, we all remember how great you are at imagining), it wasn't easy inflating the pig bladders, so they were often left unevenly filled. That was great for the Tom Bradys of the day (see "The New England Patriots, filthy cheaters"), but few others. So, like all great technology eventually does, footballs moved away from being bladder-based.

Today's balls are made from leather or cowhide. Thus, calling a modern football a "pigskin" is not only wrong but, if overheard by a referee, subject to a fifteen-yard penalty for historical inaccuracy.

If you're reading this and are a young cow with a dream of making it into the league, just know it won't be easy. You'll have to eat a lot, and focus. Then, if luck goes your way, you'll be killed, your hide tanned in Chicago, and then sewn into a football in Ohio. If all that happens, one day you could feel the thrill of being a shanked punt as your parents proudly watch from the stands where they've been made into stadium hamburgers and hot dogs.

DAN Dan, here: We can't say for sure that *actual* beef is mixed in with the sawdust used to make stadium hamburgers and hot dogs. Our lawyers insist we note that "it's possible, but not a certainty."

In the Beginning, There Was the Creation of Earth, and Waaaaay After That . . . Football

DAN It may seem logical that pro football is the reason college ball exists, with college ball serving as the place aspiring young athletes showcase their skills in exchange for an education they'll never need if they've showcased their skills well enough. But thinking the pros are the reason for the college game is totally wrong. So wrong that if you time-traveled back to the late 1870s when football in America began, and told people that, they'd all think you were stupid. (After they finished calling you stupid, there'd probably be a bunch of other questions like "How'd you manage to travel through time, anyway?" and "Why does a cell phone need three camera lenses?" and "What is a cell phone and why do you keep looking at it every two minutes?")

In fact, college football existed way *before* pro football and is responsible for much of the game's evolution and innovations. So, how did football come to be played at American colleges in the first place? What a convenient and timely question!

European football, the game Americans ignore as "soccer," was being played in England as early as 1519. It was even boring then, in an era when a fly landing on an apple core was considered high entertainment. (Pretty sure *Fly Landing on Apple Core* swept the 1519 Oscars.) But it was soccer's monotony that we have to thank for football; it was so boring, people started changing it, trying to make it entertaining. One big change occurred in 1823 at Rugby School when they let players pick up the ball and run with it. This modified game was then called "rugby," just like the gameshow *Deal or No Deal* was named that after being first played at Deal or No Deal University (a Pac-10 school).

Obviously, rugby is still around today, but it also isn't popular with Americans, who love its violence but can't forgive how high the players have their socks pulled up.

Rugby made its way onto this side of the pond and was being played in American colleges by the late 1800s. It kept changing and evolving, and in 1875, when Harvard played Tufts, "modified rugby" was already looking like today's football: eleven men per side, the ball moved by kicking or carrying it, and, when a player was tackled, play was stopped. Also like today's football, that 1875 matchup featured a beer vendor who was never in your section when you were thirsty.

"Modified rugby" kept spreading, just like the most ambitious viruses, and ultimately found Walter Camp, a man so instrumental in shaping the game that he's been called "the father of football." The announcement of his fatherhood came in pretty undramatic fashion, being based on his contributions instead of by reading paternity test results live in front of a gasping audience on one of the many late 1800s reality shows.

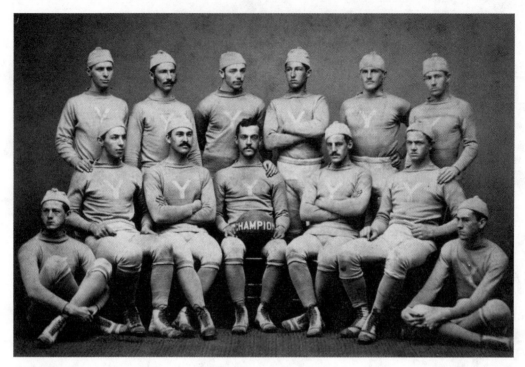

This photo is

» the 1876 Yale Bulldogs with Walter Camp (standing, arms crossed).

» a support group for a friend with a rare disease that makes your crotch swell and read "Champion."

» a math nerd's cool (but not well-coordinated) idea for his buddies to wear clothes spelling "algebraically."

» none of the above, but two other things.

DAN As college football grew in popularity, it was only a matter of time before money entered the picture, just like what happened with all the really great clog dancing websites (loudandclumsy.com, stompapalooza.com, and so on).

It happened in 1892. That's when football became a paid gig for the first time when William "Pudge" Heffelfinger and Ben "Sport" Donnelly each received cash to play for the Allegheny Athletic Association of the Western Pennsylvania Circuit (or, as no one called it, "The AAA of the WPC"). These associations organized "amateur" teams to play "exhibitions" for the love of the game but were fueled by gamblers who bet on them for their love of money.

Pudge and Sport were trailblazers for more than just getting paid for football. With that cruel nickname, Pudge became the first recorded victim of fat-shaming. After his career was over, in a touching tell-all memoir, he told the world, "Sure, money is great, but it can't buy un-hurt feelings."

Ben "Sport" Donnelly was the first to show us you can never be too lazy in assigning a nickname. By accepting "Sport" for a person who played sports, Ben bravely set an early nickname rock bottom. Without his sacrifice, guys named Mike would never be "Mikey," Daves never "Davey," and players with the initials T.O. could never be "T.O." So, a tip of the hat to "Sport" Donnelly—or as he's now known in heaven, "Dead Guy" Donnelly—for easing all our creative burdens.

Even though the game had now gone "pro," it still was only played regionally through the early twentieth century, with teams within a state only playing each other, and no national tournament to bring state champs

Walter Camp

A player at Yale before becoming the coach, he's given credit for establishing the line of scrimmage, snapping the ball, downs, the size of the field, blocking defenders, two points for a safety, and field goals. Even more impressive, as a coach his record was seventy-nine wins, five losses, and three ties. Even the coach of the Harlem Globetrotters has a worse record than that.

together. The Utah Cheaters revealed the flaws in this system by becoming a team on January 3, 1896, then, when Utah became a state the very next day, declaring themselves state champions without ever playing a game. That shameful act is why Utah still doesn't have an NFL team. Some people say the NFL has been unfairly harsh on the Beehive State, but others ask, "How else are they ever going to learn?"

It wasn't long until efforts arose to establish a countrywide league. In 1902, "The World Series of Pro Football" began, yet mysteriously and *ignorantly* only featured teams from New York and New Jersey. The league did accomplish one notable feat: playing the first-ever indoor football games in Madison Square Garden (tickets went for the usual $175). The World Series of Pro Football lasted only two seasons, which is bad, yet is still two seasons longer than the failed reality show *So You Think You Can Dentist*.

With efforts being made to start professional leagues, other efforts were also being made to end football altogether. Wearing uniforms with almost no padding and enduring constant violent scrums, players were actually dying. In 1904, eighteen players died and another nineteen died the next year. At the time, senseless deaths were frowned upon, and colleges started dropping the game or demanding changes. In response, a slate of new rules was agreed on, including the legalization of the forward pass, which, the hope was, would force players to spread out and consequently make the game safer. (Prior to this, players could only pass the ball backward, which is almost the opposite of forward. Don't believe me? Ask a scientist.)

A volunteer "tests" a leather helmet by running into a wall in 1912. The volunteer later also "sampled" a concussion, then "test-drove" a hospital bed.

Passing grew in usage and, to facilitate it, the ball was made gradually narrower until it became a "prolate spheroid." (That's only its legal name on documents and passports. Around friends, it prefers to be called "oval.")

One school that really embraced throwing the ball was the Carlisle Indian Industrial School, home to two icons of the game: Coach Glenn "Pop" Warner and his star running back, Jim Thorpe.

Jim Thorpe

Widely recognized as one of the 100 greatest players of all time, he not only played football *and* baseball, but he also won two Olympic gold medals. Once, after having a ninety-two-yard touchdown run called back by a penalty, he ran for a ninety-seven-yard touchdown on the next play. Following inane logic, if that play were also called back, he would have then scored a 102-yard touchdown, then a 107-yarder, and, at some point, a 2,005,542-yarder!

NOTE: Jim Thorpe was a very influential figure in the game, and we're going to be mentioning him repeatedly. We just want to be upfront about it. Honesty is key to any relationship.

Someone Tries Throwing the Ball

The first forward pass was thrown in a college game in September 1906. Just one month later, on October 27, 1906, the first professional completion happened in an Ohio League game, when George "Peggy" Parratt of Massillon threw to Dan "Bullet" Riley of Benwood-Moundsville. We don't have time or space to dig into why George's nickname was "Peggy," but it's safe to assume it was the result of a lost bar bet.

Glenn "Pop" Warner

Credited with creating the "modern game of football," he invented single and double wing formations, the three-point stance, the bootleg, the reverse, screen passes, and even huddles. Disputing the rumors, he is *not* credited with inventing memory foam mattresses or the OkCupid dating site.

Over his forty-nine-year career, Warner coached at Iowa State, the University of Georgia, Cornell, Carlisle, the University of Pittsburgh, Stanford, Temple, and San Jose State. So, sure, the guy's a legend, but he also clearly had a hard time holding down a job. (Apparently, a lot of it had to do with his "attitude" about washing his coffee mug in the office kitchen.)

The movement to establish a multi-state pro football league gained momentum after a rare 1917 interstate game. The Rochester Jeffersons had traveled to play against the Canton Bulldogs and their star—Jim Thorpe, who was now playing pro. (Told you we'd mention him again. If we hadn't said anything, think how awkward this would be now.) Rochester lost that game 41-0, but, as any doctor will tell you, "When your butt gets kicked, your eyes get opened." The Rochester owner suggested to Thorpe the idea of a nationwide league, similar to what baseball had already created. There was interest, but unfortunately before it could lead to anything, World War I and a flu pandemic pushed back those plans.

The league that would eventually become the NFL wouldn't be conceived until 1920. Like most conceptions, it happened in a car dealership in Canton, Ohio.

Picking a Favorite NFL Team

CHUCK TATHAM

Like middle schoolers with their faces pressed against a frosted department store window, wishing for toys they can only fantasize about (in a world where department stores still exist and middle schoolers still want toys and last week my twelve-year-old didn't sneak off with my Amex and blow six grand on crypto), Canadians like myself can only dream of having a hometown NFL team. Yes, being a football fanatic in the Great White North means *choosing* an NFL team to be your fav, and if you commit to a Cincinnati Bengals tattoo on your ass, you'd better be fully onboard.

Alas, I've never had any connection to Cincinnati (and I already have a giant birthmark on my left butt cheek that looks like a pineapple smoking a cigar), so when I was a kid growing up in Listowel, Ontario, the logical choice was either the Detroit Lions or the Buffalo Bills, because my home was equidistant from both teams. Now, you might not remember when currently resurgent Buffalo was merely mediocre. And you might not remember that Detroit has an NFL team. But when I was knee-high to someone whose knee was level with the top of my head, they were both dreary franchises, and choosing between them was like deciding between getting a cavity filled and eating cauliflower—except without the delicious hot cheese sauce. (Was it just my dentist who used delicious hot cheese sauce?)

Detroit did have fun players like Luther Blue and Lem Barney and Sheets "Sheets" Sheets and Fancypantaloons "Dave" Burns . . . and Buffalo invented chicken wings, which are mighty tasty, but very messy to eat even if you're not getting a haircut . . . but I didn't *like* the Lions or the Bills. Neither team gave me that warm, fuzzy feeling you get when you're wrapped in a big blanket, drinking hot cocoa, sitting on the curb watching your house burn down because you left the soldering gun you use to repair *Star Wars* figurines on a blanket and in a matter of minutes it turned the bungalow your dad built with his own hands into a smoldering heap of charred memories. So, I went off the board and chose a third team.

Then I found out that Blue Oyster Cult was a progressive rock band and not the previous year's AFC West champ, so I was back to square one. Square One was a summer mall outside Listowel. (For those not familiar with the term, a "summer mall" is a mall that's closed from October to April because the roof blew off, and in the winter the mall fills with snow and elk and circus people "between jobs.") I'd go to Square One to hang out at the candle store with the other cool kids, to basically just be "me" without the pressure of always being "on" and "popular" and using quotation "marks" correctly. One Saturday in 1979, a couple of days before the mall was scheduled to shut down for winter (the candle store was already ankle-deep with slush), a jersey in the window of a sporting goods store caught my eye.

It was a jersey of shimmering purple and gold, with a little sign in front of it with one simple word: "Vikings." The Minnesota Vikings: a team I'd never given much thought, but that day—as I stared at those glorious colors, the mall snow swirling around my head—I realized I'd found my beloved.

The Purple People Eaters played outside in arctic Metropolitan Stadium, and committing my allegiance to this frigid franchise made perfect sense because we had so much in common. They were a cold-weather team; I slept naked with my window open. The Vikings' coach was Bud Grant; my Aunt Glenda drank Bud Light for breakfast. The Vikings' colors were purple and gold; Aunt Glenda's legs were purple and gold. And the Vikes had lost in the Super Bowl like fifty-three times, so it was only a matter of time until the Vince Lombardi Trophy went to the Twin Cities.

Yes, from that day forward, I wouldn't be just a balding teenager with an extensive shoplifting record whose dad hadn't talked to him since the fire.

I'd be a winner.

Except in the more than four decades since that blustery day, the Minnesota Vikings haven't been back to the Super Bowl once, let alone won it. Not a single appearance over that long, wretched expanse of time—years where I eventually lost all my hair, got a hairpiece, lost the hairpiece on a rollercoaster at Six Flags over Saskatoon, and purchased another hairpiece with GPS sewn into it so I would never lose it again. During those years, McDonald's served more than ninety-one billion hamburgers, there were twelve *Croods* sequels, and the Vikings appeared in as many Super Bowls as Blue Oyster Cult. In this "Distal Era," as I call it (because the Vikings have been pretty dismal, and for a long time, I confused the word "distal" with the word "dismal"), two especially distal moments stand out:

THE NFC Championship Game Against the Atlanta Pooheads

January 1999 was notable for two reasons: one, I quit my job because of anxiety (I was a bouncer in a biker bar called "Slugfest" where any customer who chugged an entire bottle of schnapps got a free baseball bat); and two, Gary Anderson was the Vikes' placekicker on a 15-1 squad that was up 27–20 late in the NFC Championship against Atlanta—and Anderson had not missed a field goal all season. Which of course meant that late in the game Anderson *did* miss a 39-yard field goal that would've sealed a 30–20 win for Minnesota and sent the Vikes to the Super Bowl, and my neighbors would have called me "Cool Vikings Guy" and not "Bald Idiot Who Accidentally Put Brake Fluid in the Bird Fountain and Wiped Out an Entire Generation of Sparrows." After the botched kick, of course Atlanta scored the tying touchdown and won in overtime, and before you could say, "Something this horrible will never ever happen to the Vikings again," I was subjected to . . .

The NFC Championship Game Against the New Orleans Turdfaces

I believe it was Hemingway who wrote, "I wished I had died before I ever loved anyone but her." And I believe it was Hemingway because I just Googled it. I also believe that I wish *I* had died before I ever loved the Vikings, especially on January 24, 2010, when Brett Favre quarterbacked my beloved team deep into New Orleans territory late in the fourth quarter, but instead of taking a knee because the game was tied and all we had to do was kick a field goal to win it and go to the Super Bowl . . . or he could've just thrown the ball into the stands because the game was tied and all we had to do was kick a field goal to win it and go to the Super Bowl . . . or HE COULD HAVE STRIPPED NAKED AND SUNG "TUBTHUMPING" BY CHUMBAWAMBA BECAUSE THE GAME WAS TIED AND ALL WE HAD TO DO WAS KICK A FIELD GOAL TO WIN IT AND GO TO THE SUPER BOWL!!!!

Instead of doing any of those things, Brett Lorenzo Favre, a Hall of Famer because of his success with the Green Bay Packers (just typing that makes me feel barfy), *threw an interception.* Yup, we gave the Saints the ball, the game went into OT, they won, and then they won the Super Bowl. Which New Orleans player made the interception doesn't matter (Tracy Porter), how much time was left is immaterial (nineteen seconds), and I actually handled it pretty well (I did a Dr Pepper spit take on Sean O'Casey, an exchange student from Dublin who was staying with us; threw a bowl of potato salad down the basement stairs; and ran into the street screaming, "Me no feel good, Mama!").

But my clearest memory of that day was when Sean O'Casey ran into the street and grabbed me by the shoulders, Dr Pepper still dripping off his forehead, and said, "It's just a bloody game! Who cares if your Vikings never win a Super Bowl? Get a new dream, like owning and operating a maternity wear store!

"My friend," I replied calmly, "there is nothing 'better' than loving the Vikes. I worship them; I will always worship them. I know you're using my toothpaste, and nothing you can say will stop me from living and dying with my Minnesota Vikings."

And with that, I turned on my heel, headed downtown, and got a Vikings tattoo on my *right* butt cheek—a tattoo I'm told is misspelled and lopsided, though of course I've never seen it. Which is sort of perfect, actually, because when you love the Minnesota Vikings, it isn't about seeing—it's about believing.

KICKOFF!

On September 17, 1920, the meeting that would lead to the founding of the NFL was being held at a Hupmobile auto showroom in Canton, Ohio. The men attending also hoped to buy Hupmobiles with rustproofing and extended warranties thrown in. Forming an iconic institution proved easier, however, since as we all know, when they "throw it in," you're paying for it somehow.

At that fateful meeting, the American Professional Football Association (APFA) was formed, featuring fourteen teams from Ohio, Illinois, Indiana, and New York.

Franchises included the Decatur Staleys (named after their owner, A. E. Staley), the Dayton Triangles (presumably their owner was a wealthy triangle, heir to the isosceles fortune), and the Racine Cardinals, a team still playing over a hundred years later as the Arizona Cardinals. This makes sense since when you get really old, you move to Arizona for the dry heat, and also so that if you eventually go to Hell, you're used to the temperature.

The APFA had its first season in 1920 and crowned its first champion: the Akron Professionals. Since players were being paid, the name "Professionals" was totally accurate. Sadly, the same can't be said about today's teams' names, where, for example, there are only a handful of actual jaguars (*Panthera onca*) on the Jacksonville Jaguars.

In these early days, change was constant, as the league shrank and grew just like that mole your dermatologist says they "want to keep an eye on."

★★★ HISTORICAL HISTORY ★★★

We Have a Winner! (For the First Time)

The league's first championship led to the NFL's first scandal (and, as far as we know, its last). The Professionals won the Brunswick-Balke Collender Cup (which had itself just won the title for "Worst Named Trophy"), but two other teams claimed *they* deserved to share the championship: the Decatur Staleys, who would one day grow up to be the Chicago Bears, and the Buffalo All-Americans, who would one day grow up to not exist. Ultimately, the league ruled that Akron would keep the title, denying Buffalo a championship quicker than Marv Levy ever would.

ARIZONA CARDINALS

FOUNDED 1920

The Cardinals play their games in State Farm Stadium, which has the catchy State Farm slogan "Like a good neighbor, we'll charge you thirty dollars to park."

A charter member of the league, they were the Racine Cardinals, the Chicago Cardinals, and the St. Louis Cardinals; then, in 1988, they moved to Phoenix. These frequent moves make sense when you learn the Cardinals have really bad credit and are dodging repo men and landlords all over the United States.

NOTABLE CARDINALS

ERNIE NEVERS—On November 28, 1929, as a Chicago Cardinal, he scored six touchdowns and *every one* of his team's forty points (no other player would score six touchdowns again until Alvin Kamara in 2020). According to historians, a Chicagoan who had Nevers on his fantasy team but didn't start him that day was "upset about it."

LARRY FITZGERALD—Widely considered by coaches, fans, and players as one of the all-time great receivers in NFL history, Fitzgerald is second in career receiving yards and receptions, and sixth in receiving touchdowns. Consequently, statistics *also* widely consider him one of the all-time greats.

KYLER MURRAY—Murray set an NFL record in 2020 for the most games with a passing and rushing TD in a single season (nine). In postgame interviews, Cardinal receivers and running backs said they were happy Murray was getting all the touchdowns and almost sounded convincing.

CHICAGO BEARS

FOUNDED 1921

Started as the Decatur Staleys, they're not just one of the oldest franchises, but also one of the most successful. The Bears can brag about having nine championships, the most players in the Hall of Fame, and more victories than any other team. This last stat is impressive until you remember the Bears have also been around the longest. It's sort of like the school janitor boasting about how he gets more minutes on the basketball court than the team's best player (then bitterly adding, "And still, not one letter from a college scout").

NOTABLE BEARS

GEORGE HALAS—Over his career, he was an owner, manager, coach, and player. He even coached a game when he was seventy-two. He managed that game and clock perfectly but was overheard complaining about a fifteen-yard penalty, saying, "You know, I remember when you could get that penalty *and* see a movie for just five yards."

RED GRANGE—Nicknamed the "Galloping Ghost" (because "Red Grange" wasn't odd enough), he signed a huge contract with the Bears in 1925 for $100,000 (that's $1.2 million today). Sadly, his employers wanted him to work for the money, once making Grange play eight games in just twelve days (that's eight games in twelve days today).

BRONKO NAGURSKI—He accomplished everything little boys dream of: Hall of Fame inductee, professional wrestler, and, in retirement, gas station owner. Legend was that if you visited his service station, you became a repeat customer—because Nagurski would screw your gas cap on so tight, no one else could unscrew it. Also because, if you went anywhere else, Nagurski would put you in a figure-four leglock.

CHICAGO BEARS

DICK BUTKUS—(If reading this to a child, for decency's sake, change his name to "Richard Bum-smooch.") One of the most intimidating linebackers in NFL history, he was part of one of the best drafts in history when, in 1964, the Bears acquired him, Gale Sayers, and some Apple stock.

GALE SAYERS—The "Kansas Comet" was, as most comets are, very difficult to tackle. He scored twenty-two TDs his rookie year and made four Pro Bowls before retiring early due to injuries. At thirty-four, he was the youngest player ever to be inducted into the Hall of Fame and is still the NFL's greatest "Gale," slightly ahead of some players' moms.

MIKE DITKA—One of only two people to ever win an NFL title as a player, assistant coach, and head coach, he was also one of only four people in modern NFL history to win as coach of the team for which they also played. Ditka was frequently referenced in the *Saturday Night Live* sketch that popularized the expression "Dah Bears." Incidentally, "Dah Bears" is also the answer to "Who Ate Dah Campers?"

WALTER PAYTON–an all-time great running back, Payton was nicknamed "Sweetness" after slipping past a college teammate in practice and yelling, "Your sweetness is your weakness!" He also reportedly yelled the same things at overly sugared drinks at the grocery store, but out of respect for his talent, the grocery clerks never mentioned it to the press.

WILLIAM "THE REFRIGERATOR" PERRY–When a player is named after an appliance, you know they aren't small–except of course for the Bengals' Sam "Hand Mixer" Jones. "The Fridge" weighed 335 pounds and was normally a defensive tackle, but he also ran in two touchdowns, and caught another one. He is to this day (although honestly, we have no idea what day you're reading this) the heaviest player to score a touchdown in the Super Bowl. He also holds another odd, useless record: the largest-ever Super Bowl ring, at size twenty-five. Most men's rings are size nine to twelve, unless, you know, you like to wear them baggy.

AARON GIBSON–He's not well known, but we've listed him here because after reading about "The Fridge," you may now wonder: Who is the heaviest NFL player ever? Gibson was, at 410 pounds. To answer the next obvious question, he would have weighed only 66.14 pounds on the moon, been considered "underweight," and probably never been drafted. So, in retrospect, Aaron, smart move choosing to play here on Earth.

The Mayor of Philadelphia Gives a Press Conference

CHRISTINE NANGLE

OFFICIAL TRANSCRIPT

Good morning.

I think we can all agree that the past twelve hours have been among our city's worst and most embarrassing—which to be honest, for Philadelphia, is quite a feat.

I'm speaking, of course, about the events following yesterday's playoff game against the Dallas Cowboys, as emotional Eagles fans filtered onto the field and into the streets after the final whistle.

Some have criticized my administration's pre-game preparations, which you should know were solidly based on documented experience. We removed trash cans from the streets, boarded the windows of businesses, and even greased metal poles to prevent hooligans with admirable upper body strength from climbing them in order to wave jerseys and shout "Woo."

Unfortunately, the accidental ingenuity of the Eagles fan knows neither bounds nor shame. Fires were started for no real reason, and they rapidly spread via the trash strewn through the receptable-free streets. Entire neighborhoods were ablaze before Quicken Loans could even name their Quicken Loans Defensive Play of the Game.

As usual, chants of "Go Eagles" were heard echoing throughout town, making it impossible for revelers to hear the people who were actually screaming "GO! SEAGULLS!"—the latter, of course, dire warnings about the descending hordes of voracious birds.

These thousands of gulls, we now know, were there to feed on the millions of flying ants—which themselves had swarmed out of the Wissahickon Valley to feed on the scrapple-brand pork grease we used to lubricate the street poles. Regrettably, it turns out, breakfast meat is quite delicious to biting insects of all kinds.

Folks who had attempted to climb the poles to get away from the many, many fires were left greased-up, ant-ravaged, and covered in seagull feathers. In an act of stunning redundancy, they were then tarred and feathered for impersonating the Eagles mascot without a license.

Back to the many fires. They would have burned far longer and more destructively if our citizens had not pried open hundreds of municipal fire hydrants. Of course, they had no idea they were helping.

Unfortunately, the boarding up of the storefronts had the unintended effect of reducing the water's drainage and effectively turning the roads into raging canals. The Delaware River rapidly overflowed, sending a riverboat casino floating down the Vine Street Expressway directly into the end zone at Lincoln Financial Field. My hearty congratulations to everyone who had that bet, which I understand paid off at +2600.

Unfortunately, at the other end zone, fans brought down the goalpost, impaling four cheerleaders plus one ninety-six-year-old war veteran who'd been fulfilling a lifelong dream of watching the game from the sidelines. In a bit of happy news, we learned from Ol' Leonard's family that his *other* lifelong dream was to be skewered in a kabob of screaming hotties, so good for him. And my congratulations to every-one who had *that* bet, which paid off north of three hundred.

As we know, one factor that incited the frenzy last night was that a referee refused to grant the Eagles a fifth down. We've all seen the harrowing video of him being dangled by spectators off the balcony of the Miller Lite Phlite Deck. Luckily his fall was broken by the Verizon Xfinity Bud Light Dunk Tank on the concourse level.

Afterward, he was placed in police custody for his own safety. A short time later, he was removed from police custody for his own safety. Just because you're a cop doesn't mean you're not a fan. He was then moved to the Immaculate Heart of Mary convent for a few hours, but someone, or should I say some *nun*, jammed a censer of burning frankincense down his throat. He is safer on the streets, and we wish him luck. But not too much.

I know you have questions about the car flipping. Frankly, I do too. Seems we can't get through one of these sports riots without it. Officers were called to a Tar-get parking lot to find every car had been flipped over by a mob that was dispers-ing out the south exit, just as yet another mob approached from the north and, heads full of car-flipping steam, flipped the vehicles back to their upright positions. So that one is kind of a wash, I guess. If only we had those folks on the offensive line last night, am I right?

I'm sad to say that one of the absurd number of fatalities includes my father-in-law, Joe. We will all remember him for his warm smile and familiar catchphrase: "Yo, let's throw snowballs at Santa." His last words were: "Youse remember when we threw snowballs at Santa?" In lieu of flowers, please throw snowballs at Santa.

I shudder to think how many more casualties there'd be had we lost the game.

Please note I've instituted an 8 PM curfew tonight, at which time Questlove has agreed to deliver a fireside chat on his Instagram Live.

Now, folks, I was here for the Tastykake drought; I held the line during the Cream Cheese Riots; I took a battery to the temple in the unrest after the Birds traded McCoy for Kiko Alonso. But what happened last night, well, I'm sure it will happen again, or worse. I can't help recalling my campaign slogan, "Philadelphia: You know we don't have to be like this, right?"

In times like these, remember, we don't need more Rocky Balboas. We need Andrew Becketts and Joe Millers—Tom Hanks's and Denzel Washington's characters from the Oscar-winning masterpiece *Philadelphia*. Quiet dignity. Let's give it a try—okay, okay, I'm sorry. I can't get through that without laughing.

Just be safe. And if anyone has any tips on how I can remove all this green paint from my face and body, let me know.

THE
192s

THE NFL AS
A STRUGGLING STARTUP

1928

The Providence Steam Rollers become the last team not currently an NFL team to capture a league title. Some have suggested that distinction actually belongs to the Detroit Lions, who last won in 1957, but that just seems hurtful and this book isn't about that. We're not sure what it is about, but probably not that.

1929

Like a burglar entering a home, or mold entering a shower, the modern world slowly creeps into the game as the same Steam Rollers become the first team to host a game at night. To help players and the 6,000 fans follow the action, the ball was painted white, making it look like a large egg. This wasn't an accident. Penny-pinching owners actually only painted one ball, which was then used alongside a dozen hard-boiled ostrich eggs. This plan seemed foolproof until a very angry mother ostrich appeared at the game. She eventually calmed down after all her eggs were returned and she was given season tickets.

DAN Like any new business, the going was tough for the APFA. Teams based in small cities like Kenosha, Racine, and Rochester couldn't generate enough financial support. Even the Canton Bulldogs, who were winning on the field (with back-to-back titles in 1922 and 1923), were struggling. To make ends meet, teams would ask players to get part-time jobs delivering ice or newspapers, or to sell selective organs. Don't worry, no one ever had to sell any "important" organs (unless they were a second-stringer—then everything was up for grabs).

The league was also struggling to establish the racism many accuse the NFL of today. In 1920, Fritz Pollard and Bobby Marshall became the first two African American players, and in 1921, before the league knew how good it could be at limiting minority coaching opportunities, Pollard became the first African American head coach. It wasn't long until the NFL found its groove, however; they avoided hiring another Black head coach until Art Shell in 1989.

Another breakthrough in diversity came when the Oorang Indians, a team based in LaRue, Ohio, joined the league. Every player was an indigenous American, including their star and coach, Jim Thorpe (yes, him again). With a population under one thousand, LarRue remains the smallest town ever to have an NFL franchise. LaRue today is still small, and, according to Google Maps, has a bait shop with an ATM inside. If you're in Ohio looking for cash and red worms, this may be just the place!

★★★ HISTORICAL HISTORY ★★★

The League Makes a Name for Itself

In 1922, the AFPA rebrands to become . . . the National Football League. (Spoiler alert: This would remain the league's name for the next 100 years.)

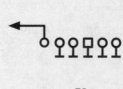

GREEN BAY PACKERS

FOUNDED 1919

Even though they were founded in 1919, the team didn't join the APFA until 1921. Because of this, Packers fans point out that they, not Chicago or Arizona, are technically the oldest NFL team, especially since they've remained in the same city for the longest time. This is correct, but, as restaurant reviewers describe the sushi at the airport, "tough crap."

There are many confusing names in the NFL. For example, what's a "Dolphin"? I guess we'll never know. We do, however, know what a "Packer" is. Many people think the name refers to how Green Bay players are famous for fitting lots of clothes into small suitcases, but the name actually dates back to Curly Lambeau who, when founding the team, was also working for a meat-packing company called "Indian Packers." The company agreed to give the team money for uniforms and a place to practice in exchange for them taking the name. Since the team is now worth an estimated $4.25 billion, it was a shrewd deal for the Indian Packing company. Or would have been, if they weren't absorbed by the Acme Packing Company, which then eventually went defunct. We'd love to detail more corporate machinations of the Midwestern meat-packing industry, but we're saving those for a much less interesting book.

GREEN BAY PACKERS

NOTABLE PACKERS

AARON RODGERS—A skilled QB, Rodgers led the team to victory at the 2011 Super Bowl. In 2021, Rodgers decided to risk all the goodwill he'd built up in a stellar career by going through protracted contract posturing, flirting with hosting *Jeopardy!* (is there a less romantic version of flirting than this?), partaking of the hallucinogenic Ayahuasca, and lying about his COVID vaccination status. Rodgers is consequently beloved, behated, and still behind much of the team's success.

REGGIE WHITE—The defensive end was selected to the NFL 75th Anniversary All-Time Team, 100th Anniversary All-Time Team, and thirteen Pro Bowls. Since he was also an evangelical minister, White was known as the "Minister of Defense." An official Pentagon statement clarified that "Mr. White never served in any official government capacity, nor did he have military clearance. The nickname was just that. A nickname." White also, of course, played for the Eagles, but we've listed him as a Packer. This will probably cause a riot in Philly; we'll happily pay all damages.

BRETT FAVRE—Favre had 321 consecutive starts from 1992 to 2010, the most in league history, and is the first quarterback with 70,000 yards, 10,000 passes, 6,000 completions, 500 touchdowns, 200 wins, and victories over all 32 teams. He's also the NFL leader in interceptions thrown and has made many questionable off-field decisions, including agreeing to play for the Jets, so he's kind of a mixed bag.

BART STARR—Starr is the only quarterback to lead a team to three consecutive championships (1965 to 1967), including the first two Super Bowls. He also has one of the highest-ever postseason passer ratings (104.8) and is one of the all-time NFL leaders in percentage of letters being "r" in a surname (40 percent).

NEW YORK GIANTS

FOUNDED 1925

When today's New York Giants formed, there was already a New York Giants baseball team, so they incorporated as the "New York National League Football Company, Inc." They changed their name to "New York Football Giants" in 1937, sending out an email asking everyone to update their contacts. Not everyone did, and to this day, when the Giants text someone, they'll often get the response "Who is this?"

The team's heated rivalry with the Eagles dates all the way back to 1933, and as of this writing, the Eagles hold a slight edge of 93–88–2. Books take a long time to be published, so maybe by the time you're reading this, the Giants have pulled ahead. Of course, there's also the chance the Eagles' lead has gotten even bigger. Thinking about the emotional risks of both, the only safe decision is to not read this book. You're still in the early part. You can probably get your money back.

NOTABLE GIANTS

(aside from André the Giant and the cartoon giant occasionally seen in TV commercials hustling frozen peas)

ELI MANNING—A member of the Manning football royal family, Eli and brother Peyton each have two Super Bowl wins and like to mercilessly remind their NFL QB dad, Archie, that "Two is two more than you'll ever have." This is usually said in a snotty voice after some dinner-table argument and leads to Eli and Peyton running to their rooms, slamming the doors, and playing music really loud.

JASON PIERRE-PAUL—A two-time Pro Bowler and Super Bowl champion with the Giants, he suffered an odd injury on July 4, 2015, when a firework blew up in his hand, leading to the loss of his index finger. With effort, Pierre-Paul recovered, and later, playing for Tampa Bay, was again a Pro Bowler and Super Bowl champion. Some attribute this later success to him being even faster without the weight of that missing finger (albeit understandably slower at texting).

NEW YORK GIANTS

LAWRENCE TAYLOR–Nicknamed "L.T." (for no known reason), he's regarded as the greatest defensive player ever. He's the only player to win Defensive Player of the Year in his rookie season, and is one of only two defensive players to ever win league MVP. (Alan Page was the other, in 1971.) L.T. was so formidable that the only thing other teams ever found could stop him was a series of deep pits dug around the quarterback, filled with crocodiles.

DAN The pits were cleverly covered with turf so they looked just like any other part of the field. Eventually, officials started to notice L.T. and other pass rushers disappearing, and at league meetings in 1996, this practice was deemed illegal.

PLAXICO BURRESS–A wide receiver, Burress caught the game-winning touchdown in Super Bowl 42. In 2008, he went to jail after shooting himself in the leg with an unpermitted gun. His claim of self-defense was unsuccessful.

MICHAEL STRAHAN—Strahan was a dominant pass rusher who currently shares (with T. J. Watt) the single-season record for sacks at 22.5. After his Hall of Fame career, Strahan decided to relax by working even harder, becoming a morning talk show host, a football analyst, a game show host, and taking a regular shift at a local Foot Locker, where he holds the record for single-day hosiery sales at 22.5 socks. He shares this record with T. J. Watt as well. Not the football player—this T. J. is a high school student who works weekends.

EMLEN "THE GREMLIN" TUNNELL—A nine-time Pro Bowler and two-time league champion, he was the first African American inducted into the Hall of Fame. Per his endorsement deals, Tunnell got a small payout anytime anyone bought an AMC Gremlin or a ticket to the 1984 movie *Gremlins*, or drove through any tunnel.

The House of DuPuy

ANDY RICHTER

I must admit I'm not a big football fan. I mean, I can enjoy almost three-quarters of a game at a friend's house, and the Super Bowl is always kind of fun, what with the nachos and the halftime pyrotechnics, but I'm an incurable smart-ass, and football guys are usually the type that bullies my type. And I'm not in the habit of accepting freelance writing assignments, because I'm lazy and also a Hollywood big shot. But when I was asked to interview Guy-Louis DuPuy of House of DuPuy, the NFL's chief costume designer for the last seventy-odd years, I jumped at the chance. Because if there's one thing I'm passionate about, it's fashion, especially fashion that's designed for men with twenty-inch necks.

It took me a while to find DuPuy's Canton, Ohio, atelier, as it's tucked in an alley behind a sausage shop and a tavern called "Not the Sausage Shop," but when I finally found it, I was rewarded with a room full of dressing dummies draped in a cacophony of color. A spry old man emerged from the mannequins, reminding me of Robert Palmer in that video with all the models made up like corpses.

In a faint French accent, he asked, "So you want to interview the man who dresses the manliest of men, eh? Well, that is me, DuPuy!" I asked him what part of France he was from, and he surprised me by telling me that he had lived in Canton his whole life. Noting my puzzlement, he said, "Oh, you mean because of my accent? Well, you see, it, like this job, is one of the many things I inherited from my father." Guy-Louis's father was the first costume designer for the nascent NFL, the founder of the House of DuPuy, and the man who single-handedly created the look we all now know as footballness.

"You know, in the early days, the game was not fully formed. They had not even invented end zones. The running back would get the ball and run off in whatever direction caught his fancy! And yet, my father knew there was tremendous potential for the game and for him to pursue his passion: dressing violent, violent men."

One of the elder DuPuy's first innovations was to replace the players' cotton or wool sweaters with canvas jerseys that had laces running up the torso. When tightened, these laced garments afforded little fabric for opposing players to grab onto, and were quickly adopted by all teams.

"The laces provided a performance advantage, but what my father really was going for was much more romantic. His heart broke at the idea of all of these men, gathering in the elements to make contact with each other, yet stymied from doing so by corseting. Reaching, grabbing, yet having the object of their desire slip away. The tragic beauty of this would cause my father to stand on the sidelines during games and loudly weep and wail. I think this may be why the league asked him to stop coming to games."

While most of DuPuy Sr.'s designs in the burgeoning years of the sport were ostensibly motivated by function, such as under-jersey shoulder pads ("My father cared very little for protection. He just wanted the boys to 'look turgid'"), the branding of teams provided ample opportunity for his creativity to shine. DuPuy's designs of the 1920s were a sensation, as he outfitted teams strictly according to their branding.

"The Bears' uniforms were made of bear hide, the Tigers' of tiger hide, and so on. You could never get away with that today, but in those days you could kill and skin pretty much whatever you wanted." Outfitting some teams was more problematic. "The Cardinals, for instance, it took at least four hundred birds to create one jersey, and the beaks would never stay on during gameplay. And I won't even get into the difficulties the Canton Bulldogs presented."

Not all of his father's designs were hits. Guy-Louis shows me an old sketch on yellowed paper, telling me it's his father's design for the short-lived team the Kenosha Dirty Foreigners. It's a bizarre mish-mash of puzzling stereotypes: the helmet a conical straw *comme les Chinois* hat with a squirrel tail hanging off the back; a long, fake, braided red beard; the jersey an embroidered smock with what look to be turnips hanging off of it; a grass skirt; and boots made to look like huge, hairy bare feet.

"It was a problem from the very beginning," Guy-Louis says, his voice halting. "The uniform made people feel very bad, a kind of bad they had never felt before. The league brought in some college professors, and they were able to put a name to the feeling. It was embarrassment, and it was the first time anyone in this country had ever felt it."

Guy-Louis took over for his father sometime in the 1950s, and he's solely responsible for how your favorite team looks today. He seems somewhat chagrined as I list some of his most brilliant innovations: The stretchy pants. The shiny pants. The stretchy shiny pants. He tells me that he is merely carrying on his father's legacy, and little more.

As he walks me to the door, I ask him if he has any design regrets, and he shakes his head. "Teal," he says. "That f**king teal."

Cowboy Cleats—'75

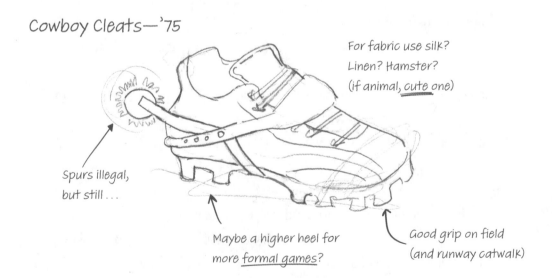

For fabric use silk?
Linen? Hamster?
(if animal, cute one)

Spurs illegal,
but still . . .

Maybe a higher heel for
more _formal games_?

Good grip on field
(and runway catwalk)

Rise Up, Kickers!

Small, sometimes European, kickers are closer to sommeliers than athletes: "Can I interest you in something onside? With hints of squib and a high bounce?"

But kickers are indeed athletes, and, as is rarely seen, they're athletes who are also geniuses. They play in the violent NFL, but it's a penalty to hit them. They have the longest careers of any position. And usually work only seconds a game. This is why high school guidance counselors hand the fragile, lazy kids brochures about careers in kicking.

But this section isn't just to praise kickers for their smarts and laziness—it's to advocate for a proper appreciation of their talents.

Question: If a field goal hits the uprights and bounces out, why doesn't it count?

A baseball hitting the foul pole counts as a home run. Why not extend the same sports courtesy to kickers? In fact, why not make kicks that hit the uprights worth *extra* points? They're very hard to hit. Following this sound reasoning, why not make bouncing the ball off the upright and then *also* going between the uprights worth, like, 100 points? Or even better, make it an automatic game winner, even if it occurs in the first minute. The refs would declare the win, confetti would be shot out of cannons, and everyone in the stands would get a free taco and the next week off work.

Sadly, the NFL would never celebrate this feat of the foot because there's a strong bias against kickers. Some call it "anti-kicker-ism," others describe it as "place-ism," and none have called it "leg-regation." Still, it exists. You know how many kickers are in the Hall of Fame? The internet does: four! You know how many offensive linemen are? Fifty-two! Offensive linemen are heavy-footed behemoths who just try to slow people down like broken subway turnstiles—and there are ten times more of them in the Hall than kickers? A travesty!

You know how many of the twenty-five all-time highest scorers in NFL history are kickers? *All of them!* We have to drop down to forty-second place to find a player who is *not* a kicker, and that's some guy named Jerry Rice no one's ever heard of.

This ignoring of foot finesse is an injustice of the highest order! It cannot stand! All you kickers out there, put this book down immediately, pick up your favorite torch and pitchfork, and let's meet to march on the Hall of Fame together!

But, kickers, we can't let the snobs in Canton see our small, European mob coming, so let's gather a few blocks away at the Groom Room Pet Spa (Broad and 21st). It's apparently also a great place to get your dog groomed—an online review says "They gave Gizmo the best cut he's ever had!"—so if you have a pet, why not bring them and kill two birds with one stone? (P.S. Let's maybe not use the expression "kill two birds with one stone" around the owners. They're probably animal lovers.)

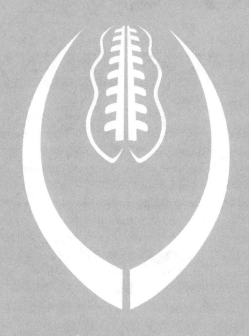

THE
1930s

THE NFL AS A TEENAGER

DAN Like all teens, the NFL continued to experience a lot of change and probably greasy skin. Teams came and went; rules evolved; the league had its first draft and first televised game. Also like a teenager, the football itself was going through body changes: to increase passing, it became tapered at the ends and thinner in the middle, and immediately started posting its "new look" on all the 1930s social media sites.

The goalposts moved from the back of the end zone to the front (for more field goals) and helmets became more protective, moving from soft leather to hard leather. In 1939, a new company called Riddell introduced a plastic helmet, and then plastic became rare during World War II. Thus, because of the war effort, safer helmets would have to wait. Yet one more thing to be furious at Nazis about.

1932

The first season that the NFL records official statistics. For a brief time before any games start, this fact serves as the only statistic.

1934

The Bears' Beattie Feathers becomes the first 1,000-yard rusher in a season. See, if they didn't have stats, he'd have just been the league's first "lotta running" rusher.

"The Sneakers Game"

(Different Than "The Snickers Game," Which Never Happened)

The 1934 Championship between the Giants and Bears is known as "The Sneakers Game." The New York Polo Grounds field was frozen, and the Giants, trailing 13–3, were having a hard time getting traction. Then someone said, "What if we wear sports shoes for this sporting event?" The Giants changed into sneakers and rallied to a 30–13 victory. Postgame, the embarrassed Giants coach admitted that even though they had an endorsement deal with a tap-dance shoe company, the team shouldn't have started the game wearing them.

1936

The Packers' Arnie Herber becomes the first 1,000-yard passer.

1936

The first NFL draft. Finally, a day when prospects find out if they get the job they've been auditioning for their whole life.

★ ★ ★ HISTORICAL HISTORY ★ ★ ★

Football History Makes Television History, and Vice Versa

On October 22, 1939, the Eagles played the Brooklyn Dodgers in the first televised NFL game (a college game had been televised a few weeks earlier). With TVs a rarity, only about 5,000 people watched, yet they all had the same reaction—"Too many beer commercials."

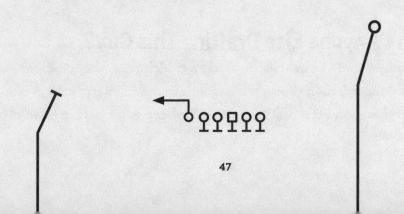

The Draft

DAN Today, the draft is a big, televised event. The obvious first-round picks show up in person so when their names are called, they can go on stage and smile next to the commissioner, knowing they're now rich and will probably never have to talk to the commissioner again.

Some draft moments worthy of being mentioned in a book (this book):

Thanks, but No Thanks

When it started, players looked at being drafted as a pleasant invitation or gentle suggestion. Of the eighty-one players selected in the very first draft in 1936, only thirty-one went on to play in the NFL. Jay Berwanger, the first player ever drafted (also the first Heisman winner), spurned the chance to play pro, instead choosing a career with a rubber company. Of course, nowadays, everyone hopes to get hired in the rubber industry with the NFL as their fallback plan, but Berwanger was way ahead of his time.

Why Isn't Anyone Else Drafting This Guy?

Everyone knows that Canada is the world's trendsetter: the most popular TikTok dances began there, putting kumquats in overpriced cocktails started there, and the first time Matt Stafford wore his baseball cap backward only happened because of a Halifax windstorm. So, as the world's trailblazer, it's not surprising that the Canadian Football League was first to draft players that were dead.

In 1995, the Ottawa Rough Riders selected Derrell Robertson in the fourth round. Unfortunately, he'd died a year before. Analysts said had Robertson not died, he might have been drafted as early as the third round. The next year, another CFL team, the Montreal Alouettes, selected James Eggink in the fifth round, who had, of course, also died. This pattern explains why there are so many CFL scouts at funerals.

If at First You Don't Succeed, Fail Again

In 1946, Washington drafted running back Calvin Rossi only to find out he was a junior in college and thus ineligible. Being rejected often makes men want something even more, so Washington drafted Rossi again the next year. This time he was eligible, but he turned the team down since he had no plans to play in the NFL (and never did). Unable to "get over it," Washington kept drafting him every year since, even after his death in 2013. Of course, once he died, the Ottawa Rough Riders and Montreal Alouettes suddenly became interested.

Cameron Jordan or Jordan Cameron?

In 2011, tight end Jordan Cameron and defensive end Cameron Jordan were both in the draft. The Browns chose Jordan Cameron, but attempting to call him, instead dialed Cameron Jordan—who had to break it to Cleveland that he'd already been picked by the Saints. The Browns called Cam

Jordanian, James Corden, and the countries of Jordan and Cameroon before finally sorting things out.

Drafted Twice (but Chose the Winning Team)

The Eagles selected Syracuse fullback Norm Michael in the 1944 draft, then learned he'd already been drafted by the U.S. Army. Michael never even knew he'd been chosen by Philadelphia until 1999, when he saw his name on a list of every drafted Syracuse player. Reading that, he showed up at the Eagles training camp in the year 2000, and was immediately hit with fines for missing fifty-five years of practice.

Mannings 2, San Diego 0

In 1998, Peyton Manning was picked first overall by the Colts, but he wasn't supposed to be. Ryan Leaf was. However, wanting to play in San Diego instead, Leaf purposely showed up to the combine overweight. The Colts got Hall of Famer Peyton and San Diego got Leaf, who was a total bust. San Diego took solace in knowing the Manning family would make it up to them in the future.

That future came in the future, when six years later, San Diego got screwed again. They drafted Eli Manning first overall, but he refused to play for them since they were . . . the Chargers. Eli was consequently traded to the Giants for their first pick, Philip Rivers. Eli won two Super Bowls while Rivers only ended up with the Chargers key chain he was given as a signing bonus.

DETROIT LIONS

FOUNDED 1930

(as the Portsmouth Spartans)

In 1934, the Spartans moved to Detroit, became the Lions, and went on to win four titles, the last in 1957. Since there's no real record of the Lions in the playoffs after this, we have to assume they stopped playing then. We could call Detroit and check, but if by chance they do still have a team, that'd be embarrassing for them and we'd feel bad. Probably better to live with our ignorance.

DETROIT LIONS

SOME LIONS' LOWLIGHTS

1970—The longest and shortest field goals ever are kicked against the Lions—in the same game!

The Saints' Tom Dempsey hits a record sixty-three-yarder against the Lions, then also kicks the *shortest* ever—just eight yards. This record can never be beaten as the goalposts have since been moved ten yards deeper in the end zone, making the shortest possible field goal seventeen yards (snap seven yards back from the goal line, then ten to the goal posts). Also, why would anyone *want* to beat this record?

2008—Detroit becomes the first team to go 0–16. (The Browns tie this embarrassment in 2017.) After the season expands to seventeen games in 2021, the Lion's head office assures fans they will try to go 0–17 and reclaim their place in infamy.

2021—Baltimore's Justin Tucker sets a new longest field goal record of sixty-six yards, also in a win over the Lions.

Look for more flashes of failure at the Detroit Lions Museum (currently closed because only one guy had a key and he lost it).

NOTABLE LIONS

BYRON "WHIZZER" WHITE–Don't let the possibly dirty nickname throw you; this may be the most accomplished "Whizzer" you know. He was a runner-up for the 1937 Heisman Trophy, a first-round draft choice, and the Lions' leading rusher for two years–granted, a tumbleweed once led the Lions in rushing (jersey now retired). "Whizzer" also went to Yale Law School and eventually became a Supreme Court justice. When he retired, he was replaced by Ruth Bader Ginsburg, who also once briefly led the Detroit Lions in rushing (jersey also retired).

BARRY SANDERS–If you've ever seen Barry Sanders run, you know his body was like a Rubik's Cube: he'd twist his hips and upper body in different directions, then reassemble once past the defenders. His moves are what kid moves want to be when they grow up. He's one of only two backs (the other is Derrick Henry) to rush for 2,000 yards in both college and the pros, and some consider him the greatest ever.

DAN Actually, an online poll ranks him number seven, but sometimes "7" and "1" get confused. For example, people think Joel has a 700 credit score.

DON MUHLBACH—For seventeen years, he was the Lions' long snapper—the specialist responsible for sending tight spirals fifteen yards backward to a waiting kicker. Muhlbach retired in 2021 yet still earns pocket money at the Detroit airport where, for five dollars, he'll "snap" your luggage into the open trunk of your car. For ten dollars, he'll snap your baby into its car seat (price varies depending on baby's weight and, oddly, middle name).

FOUNDED 1932

(as the Boston Braves)

In 1936 they changed their name to the "Redskins," in 1937 moved to Washington, in 2020 renamed themselves the "Washington Football Team," and in 2022 became the "Commanders." Each of these name changes is annoying, but also an opportunity for the team to sell merchandise with the new name. This is the exact same reason why, in 1935, the country "Persia" changed its name to "Iran."

The problematic name "Redskins" is addressed on page 57, but let's note that once Washington finally made a change, they first chose the least interesting name ever: the "Washington Football Team." This commitment to blandness was going to be followed by renaming their stadium to "Place Football Played Field," but "Guy Owning Team" and "Manager Managing Team" couldn't agree.

NOTABLE WASHINGTON PLAYERS

JOE THEISMANN—Washington's all-time leading passer took them to two Super Bowls, winning one. In 1985, on Monday Night Football, Lawrence Taylor sacked Theismann, breaking his leg in a gruesome, career-ending injury. Bad luck later struck again when Theismann was working as a color commentator for Monday Night Football. Bumped from his blind side by cohost Mike Tirico, Theismann's coffee mug fell to the ground, breaking in three places and sadly ending the coffee mug's career.

DARRELL GREEN—The longest-tenured Redskin of all time (twenty seasons), he's considered one of the greatest cornerbacks ever. Green, who was 5'9", referred to himself as an "itty bitty guy," though doctors say, medically, that term actually only refers to people under 5'7".

THE "HOGS"—A nickname given to the offensive line (average weight: 270 pounds) that helped win three Super Bowls during the 1980s and '90s. They're all retired now, enjoying life as bacon and/or glazed hams.

So, Your Team Had to Make a Change

DONICK CARY

Over the last several years, fans of the NFL franchise in Washington, DC, like myself, have had to do some serious soul-searching about the name of our beloved team. The franchise has, of course, landed on a new name: "Commanders." *Commander* is defined as a person in authority, especially over a body of troops or a military operation. Which sounds kind of good. And then they pluralized it because the team has more than one person on it, of course . . . so it is a team of commanders . . . all commanding over each other for maximum command as they go to battle on the gridiron against a variety of birds, animals, and random other things like Packers. (I think they pack cheese, right?)

As the team did their research for a good new name, I did my own, and as good and intimidating as a squad of Commanders all coming at you at once commanding each other might be, I think I might have some better ideas for a replacement for the previous offensive team name. And since the team is changing their name, on average, every two years, I'm hoping they consider some of these for their next name.

First, a few tips on finding a new name:

1. The team name doesn't need to honor anyone. The Eagles don't honor eagles. The Giants don't honor very big people. The Browns don't celebrate the color brown. (Great color, though—easily top ten!) The

name should just be cool, and the team should focus on football and specifically winning football games.

2. After doing deep dives into the subject with a huge variety of Native Americans, I think it's smart to move away from Native American imagery completely. That era is over. Chiefs and Braves, you're on the clock. Sorry, I know it's hard. But we went through it in Washington. We're still alive. It's okay to change. Plus, if you feel strongly about still honoring Native Americans, it'd be cool if you did! It'd be cool to honor Native Americans during halftime shows no matter what your team name is—like all teams do with our military. By the way, you can honor other people besides Native Americans. Why not honor working moms or doctors or just random great Washingtonians like Dave Grohl and Dave Chappelle? Maybe the team should just be the Washington Daves? Hmm. There are 10,905,563 Davids in the United States alone . . . nice fan base to tap. Could sell *a lot* of T-shirts.

3. Pick something that celebrates the team's heritage . . . not someone else's. Make football fun again, please! "The Hogs," for example, could have been badass and fun. It would celebrate the team's history, with almost zero chance of protest—except maybe from vegetarians. But in a way you'd be humanizing pigs, so you might even get their support.

Anyway—here are some of my favorite new names for the team when some-day they inevitably decide to change Commanders to something cooler.

Imagine that scary blood elevator music from *The Shining* filling the stadium as **The Washington Red-Rums** take the field. Instead of tomahawk chops, the fans all do that Danny finger thing and chant "Red-Rum, Red-Rum" over and over. When the visiting team lines up across the ball, they suddenly notice that our helmet logo, when read backward, says, "Murder"! Wait a minute, that's not Burgundy . . . that's *bloood*! No visiting team gets out alive.

I know what you are saying—you love *The Shining* thing, but don't want to pay for the rights to "Red-Rum." I think you could probably get around the copyright stuff by just going with **The Washington Dead-Twins.** If I was Rowdy, the Cowboys mascot, I wouldn't want to wrestle with that mascot on the sideline!

Let's go in another direction for a minute: classic rock.

First choice would be **The Grateful Dead-Skins**. Great imagery for logos!

The band sold out RFK Stadium more than the team sells out FedExField. Flashback tie-dye weekend alternative uniforms would be freaky cool. And talk about non-partisan: everyone from Al Franken and Nancy Pelosi to Tucker Carlson and Steve Bannon are Dead Heads. Plus, it keeps the rivalry with the Cowboys alive and well. To loosely quote their song "Me and My Uncle": "Texas Cowboy? I left his dead ass there by the side of the road."

Or let's go another classic rock route for a minute . . . **The Red Zeppelins**? There's no better song to enter a stadium to than "Rock and Roll." It's pretty insane that Led Zeppelin wrote a rock 'n' roll song and then named it "Rock and Roll" . . . that's a real rock 'n' roll move. And that's the kind of attitude our team could have. Plus, imagine a stadium full of people banging their heads with devil horns raised. And whenever we play the Dolphins? Isn't there some Led Zeppelin story about a dolphin or something? I don't know.

Classic cinema fan? Here's a suggestion: **The Washington Bill and Ted-Skins**. I don't know what this would look like on game day . . . but it sounds pretty fun. Though the team would have a lot of pressure to be "Excellent" and that's been a tough metric for the last twenty years or so.

And finally, my son Otis's vote: **The Washington Simpsons.** You'd have to give Disney at least a 40 percent ownership stake, but eventually they'll own all the content in the universe. Why delay the inevitable?

Go, team. Whatever you are!

PITTSBURGH STEELERS

FOUNDED 1933

(as the Pirates)

They changed their name in 1940, but no matter what they call themselves, they're one of the most successful franchises. They've won six Super Bowls and given us iconic moments like the "Immaculate Reception" (more on this later) and the "Immaculate Extension" (nothing on this later).

NOTABLE STEELERS

THE "STEEL CURTAIN"—The defensive line in the 1970s that helped win four Super Bowls in six years. Many fans, in tribute, outfitted their homes with actual steel curtains, immediately broke their curtain rods, and unsuccessfully sued the team.

"MEAN" JOE GREENE—A ten-time Pro Bowler, Greene wasn't "mean," just upset about how many American manufacturing jobs were being sent overseas.

ROD WOODSON—Holds the NFL record for fumble recoveries by a defensive player (thirty-two) and interceptions returned for touchdown, also, not surprisingly, by a defensive player (twelve).

TROY POLAMALU—Won two Super Bowls and was involved in both the NFL's biggest blowout—when he tried something "different" with his legendary hair—and the NFL's biggest upset—when the blowout didn't turn out how he'd hoped.

TERRY BRADSHAW—Iconic QB who threw what became the "Immaculate Reception," Bradshaw currently enjoys a career as a broadcaster, actor, and star of his own reality show, yet through it all, he remains incredibly bald.

PHILADELPHIA EAGLES

FOUNDED 1933

(sort of)

In 1933, the Frankford Yellow Jackets went bankrupt and savvy investors in Phila-delphia snapped them up and called them the Eagles, a team founded via a repos-session. They've won three NFL Championships and one Super Bowl. They have rivalries with the Giants, Cowboys, Commanders, and Steelers, so pretty much have a hard time getting along with anyone.

NOTABLE EAGLES

BRIAN DAWKINS—A Hall of Fame safety, he also co-created a hoagie sandwich called "The Dawk." If you're wondering if it has grilled chicken, Parmesan cheese, spinach, tomato, pickles, sweet peppers, and yellow mustard in it, we can report that yes, it does.

CHUCK BEDNARIK—Nicknamed "Concrete Charlie," in 1960 he hit the Giants' Frank Gifford so hard, he knocked him out of football for eighteen months. Gifford had "no hard feelings" . . . at least until doctors restored sensation to his nerves, at which point he was able to feel "very angry."

HAROLD CARMICHAEL—A Hall of Fame receiver, he was a four-time Pro Bowler and an All-Pro in 1973. If you're wondering what the difference is, stop wondering because here's the answer: "All-Pros" are the very best individuals at their position, with "Pro Bowler" a designation given to many players at a single position who get invited to the Pro Bowl. This means that even at the Pro Bowl, there's a depth chart, and if players don't perform, they can be downgraded to the Mediocre Bowl.

LOS ANGELES RAMS

FOUNDED 1936

(as the Cleveland Rams)

They won the 1945 NFL Championship in Cleveland, and then, just like LeBron taught us, realized it's okay to leave Cleveland after winning. In 1946, they moved to Los Angeles, becoming the first NFL team on the West Coast. In 1994, they moved again, to St. Louis, eventually winning the Super Bowl in 2000, and in 2016 moved back to LA, where they won the 2022 Super Bowl. The only team to win in three different cities isn't done yet: the Rams are currently meeting with realtors in Boise, Idaho.

NOTABLE RAMS

DICK "NIGHT TRAIN" LANE—Lane still holds the record for most interceptions in a season (fourteen). He earned his nickname dancing to a teammate's record of "Night Train." Luckily, his teammate wasn't a fan of Fergie, or the Hall of Fame would be home to Dick "My hump, my hump, my hump, my lovely lady lumps" Lane.

ERIC DICKERSON—Holds the season rushing record of 2,105 yards, which he set in 1984. One of the few NFL players who wore glasses while he played, Dickerson was a hero to "four-eyes" everywhere, as well as to "two-eyes" and even some "three-eyes" (people who wear monocles).

KURT WARNER—An NFL Cinderella, Warner was stocking groceries in Iowa when he got a chance to play in the Arena Football League, then climbed the football ladder to eventually win the Super Bowl with St. Louis's "Greatest Show on Turf." He's considered the best undrafted player ever and a mediocre grocery clerk.

ELROY "CRAZYLEGS" HIRSCH—Played for Chicago and Los Angeles in the 1940s and '50s, winning a championship and breaking multiple records. His nickname referred to his running style, but we're glad to report that after years of therapy, his legs went on to live a normal life, functioning like any sane pair of legs.

Rules Are Made to Be Broken

(and Penalties Are Made to Be Called When That Happens)

The average NFL game lasts three hours and twelve minutes, exactly as long as a rush-hour drive in Los Angeles. And like a rush-hour drive in LA, things are only actually moving for eleven minutes. The rest of the time is pretty much just players standing around, watching officials call and explain penalties.

Often fans don't even know what the refs are signaling, like with these:

This signifies either a touchdown or that a Wild West outlaw has his gun pressed into the official's back and wants him to hand over his flags "nice and easy-like."

Here, the lineman is suggesting the scorer keep the clock rolling *or* is describing a huge circle he caught fishing. Of course, like most fishermen and officials, he is a liar.

This isn't even a sign. This official was suspected of being drunk on the job and is being forced to walk along the thirty-yard line to prove his sobriety.

The Most Penalized Game Ever

On average, there are twelve penalties every game, but some have more. Lots more. The most penalized game ever was Cleveland versus Chicago in 1951. Thirty-seven flags were thrown for 374 yards in penalties. The game's leading quarterback, Otto Graham of the Browns, only passed for 277 yards, which explains why the referee, with all his successful flag-throwing, was declared MVP. He graciously accepted the prize of a Corvette filled with exotic figs. We've heard he still has the figs but sold the Corvette.

DAN We all agree penalties are a giant mess. The good news is this book is meant to clean up messes (for example, spills: the pages are *very* absorbent).

So, let's fix the problems with penalties, in three easy steps:

1. Not Just Fewer Penalties, but Also, *Fewer* Penalties

Holding, clipping, unsportsmanlike conduct, poor penmanship—all these terms start to lose meaning, just like other overused terms like "I love you" and "Run, fire!" So why not have just one catch-all term for all penalties? I agree, it is a great idea. The question then is, "What term?" This isn't something we wanted to half-ass, so with full-ass effort, we polled intellects, poets, and a lost tourist, and found the perfect answer:

"Oopsie."

Yes, from now on, all penalties should be called "Oopsies." Instead of some indecipherable arm movement, refs will signal an oopsie has occurred with a whistle and rubbing one index finger perpendicular to the other in the universal "shame on you" gesture.

Fans will know a penalty happened, the player will know, the ball will be moved, and the game will continue—without all the labeling. I agree, it is genius. Even more genius, this doesn't need to be reserved just for football. It could also fix the court system, with defendants standing trial for civil oopsies, intent to oopsie, aggravated oopsie, first-degree oopsie, and so on.

2. On Top of Fewer Penalties, How About *Fewer* Penalties?

Refs should call only the most egregious fouls, knowing the small stuff will even itself out over the course of the game. If that offends purists, here's another option: bribery.

It would work like this: Each team gets $1,000 in cash at the beginning of every game. The quarterback can keep it in that little tube they wear on their waists to warm their hands. As the game progresses, different amounts of cash can be slipped to officials to "overlook" things. More for something major, less for something inconsequential. Offensive pass interference that negated a touchdown? The QB could hand the ref a couple hundred and slyly say, "Why don't you go buy yourself a pretty new shirt—maybe something striped?" The ref would take the money, pick up the flag, and the game would move on. Like everything in the NFL, the bribes could be sponsored. There could be on-screen graphics like "This corruption brought to you by Secure-Fast Envelopes—doesn't your bribe deserve the best?"

3. Fewer Penalties? How About Only Two?

What if each ref was only given two flags per game, and once a flag was thrown, it couldn't be picked up? (Don't worry, the flags would be biodegradable—whatever that means.) With a maximum of only two calls every game, refs would need to pick their spots and make 'em count. Knowing this, is a ref really gonna call offsides? Sure, that might have been a cheap hit, but was it the *cheapest* hit? Even better, once players see both flags have been thrown, the field would become a lawless wasteland, like if Mad Max had been made commissioner. Isn't this the exact scenario Raiders fans keep dressing for?

While we're fixing things, there's one rule that always infuriates fans: the one determining what a "catch" is. Thankfully, we fix that next.

Thank God for the Catch Rule

ZACH POSNER AND DANIEL FURLONG

A wide receiver leaping impossibly high, twisting his body at an insane angle and snatching a football out of midair, is one of the most exciting moments in sports.

Or at least, it should be.

We know we saw the player make a gravity-defying move to *get to* the football, but are we absolutely positive he actually *caught* it? Thankfully, after more than 100 years of not being 100 percent sure, the NFL has perfected the breathtaking experience of watching these amazing feats by stopping the game, reviewing the play over and over like it's the Zapruder film, then having a referee tell you on a screechy microphone if the player caught it or not.

So breathe easy, fellow fans—you can now be painstakingly sure that each and every catch is perfectly in line with the most heart-pounding text in sports: the NFL rule book.

But what about some of your favorite plays from seasons past? Are you nervous that you may have idiotically cheered for a non-catch? Don't worry, we spent the last three years studying the minute details of what constitutes a catch in the NFL, and we're on a mission to go back and fix those feeble-eyed referees' greatest blunders.

OBJ's One-Handed Grab—November 23, 2014

Sure, we all *think* we saw Odell Beckham Jr. leap backward, catch the ball with one hand, and miraculously hold on to it as he landed in the end zone. But shame on you for living in the moment and acting like you just experienced one of the most exciting plays in sports history. Taking into account the Earth's rotation and applying Foucault's principle, the ball in OBJ's hand is clearly moving ever so slightly as he hits the ground, making it extremely incomplete! Nice try, OBJ, but maybe go back to LSU and take a frickin' physics class if you want to score an all-time great TD on our watch!

"The Catch"—January 10, 1982

"The Catch"? More like "The Definitely Not a Catch." With fifty-eight seconds left in the game and San Francisco down by six, Joe Montana scrambles to the right and chucks it up, and Dwight Clark makes the historic "catch" that sparks one of the greatest dynasties in sports history. But watch it again. Clark, pumped up by the stadium full of screaming fans, spikes the ball in celebration—clearly not maintaining possession for the requisite 247 seconds. As every kid who ever played catch with his pops in the backyard knows, if you don't hold onto the ball for the amount of time it takes to change a tire, it ain't a catch.

"The Immaculate Reception"—December 23, 1972

The "Immaculate Reception"? More like "Upon Further Review, the Pass Is Ruled an Immaculate Incompletion." When Terry Bradshaw's pass is broken up by Jack Tatum, Franco Harris comes out of nowhere, snags the deflected ball, and runs into the history books. Or does he? We sent the footage to our nation's top forensic scientists, and after six weeks and $750,000 in testing, they concluded that it is clear as day that an eighth of a millimeter of a blade of grass touches the ball as Franco Harris "catches" it. Not so immaculate, if you ask us. The pope should be ashamed!

We hope our overdue diligence will help true fans of football sleep better at night. And we want to say thank you to the NFL Rules Committee for finally making the game into one people truly want to watch. Also, please consider our plea to allow DNA evidence to be used when judging who caught a 50/50 ball.

DAN So there you have it, we fixed penalties, we fixed catches, and . . .

(PHONE RINGS)

DAN: Uh, hello?

VOICE: Hey, Dan, Steven here. Longtime listener, first-time caller. 6'1", 220 pounds.

DAN: Caller? You're calling in? How do you call in to a book?

VOICE: I dialed, talked to the guy, waited on hold for a looooong time, and now I'm here. Anyway, I want to talk about the Saints and Chris Olave—

DAN: Wait, let me stop you. This isn't happening. Calling into a book isn't a real thing.

VOICE: That sucks. Do I at least get a T-shirt or something?

DAN: We don't have T-shirts because . . . this is a book. Hey, listen, thanks, Steven, but I have to hang up.

VOICE: How can you hang up if I didn't call in? Boom—caught you in your own lie. That should be worth two T-shirts.

DAN: Right, uh . . . Well, uh . . .

(DIAL TONE)

THE
194⬤s

FIGHTING AGAINST THE WAR

DAN Some BREAKING NEWS (a book is clearly the best way to break news): There was a war in the 1940s. A pretty big one. When they give out the Biggest War Awards, World War II is definitely gonna be nominated and has a strong chance to win. Sure, it's a sequel, but some sequels are better than the original: *The Dark Knight*, *Paddington 2*, RG3 (no one ever talks about RG1 or RG2).

The war affected both the world and the world of football. With young men fighting in exotic places like Japan and Italy, it became harder to put rosters together in exotic places like Green Bay. Some teams even had to merge:

In 1943, the Steelers and Eagles merged, becoming the Phil-Pitt Steeler-Eagles (known to fans as the Steagles).

In 1944, the Chicago Cardinals and Steelers did the same thing, becoming Card-Pitt (known derisively as the Carpets).

In 1945, the Brooklyn Tigers and Boston Yanks combined to become the Yanks. A little less originality in the name here. I guess everyone in marketing had been drafted.

None of those combos lasted, since marriage across cultures is always hard. How do you raise the kids?

1940

The NFL Championship game ends in the most lopsided victory ever as the Bears humiliate Washington 73–0. Other teams in the league feel horrible having points when Washington has none, and send whatever points they can spare to the DC area.

1943

Washington's Sammy Baugh accomplishes a feat equaled only one other time: he leads the league in an offensive category (passing), a defensive category (interceptions), and a special teams category (punting). Three years later, Bill Dudley of the Steelers leads in offensive rushing, defensive interceptions, and special teams' punt return average, but not being first, no one cares. The chance to repeat this achievement ends once players specialize in just offense or defense. Wonder when that happened? Let's hope the next entry in this book talks about it!

1945

Teams begin using separate players for offense and defense. (We hoped the book would tell us when, and then it did! Thanks, Santa!)

Specifically, the first time occurred in a college game between Michigan and Army. Army had a powerful roster thanks to so many recruits going through West Point, and the Michigan coach thought his only chance was to wear down Army with fresh players on offense and defense. This "Platoon" system was mocked, but like other army inventions (radar, Silly Putty, "Don't ask, don't tell") it soon became ubiquitous.

★★★ HISTORICAL HISTORY ★★★

1945—World War II Ends!

Nowadays, instead of big world wars, we have smaller local franchises—there may even be one near you!

1946

Just like Germany split into two after the war, so are American football fans' options, as a new competitor to the NFL begins: the All-America Football Conference (AAFC).

The AAFC had teams in Chicago, Brooklyn, Buffalo, Miami, and New York, a team in Cleveland called "the Browns" (the Rams had moved to LA), one in San Francisco called the 49ers, and a team oddly called the "Los Angeles Dons."

DAN Every player on the Dons was named "Don." Made the draft difficult, but winners find a way.

By bringing football to new cities, the AAFC was credited with creating nationwide interest. To NFL owners' dismay, the competition for players drove up salaries, but to owners' un-dismay, it also drove up attendance.

1948

Los Angeles Rams halfback Fred Gehrke paints horns on his helmet and the Rams become the first team with helmet emblems. The Fargo Grass Stains have argued *they* were first to have branded helmets, but historians point out theirs were merely a product of coincidence and infrequently done laundry.

1949

The NFL realizes they love competition, just not against them. They thus agree to merge with the AAFC, bringing in the Browns, the 49ers, and the Baltimore Colts (who had replaced the Miami team).

NOTE: The above-mentioned Colts only lasted one year before folding, so they shouldn't be confused with the Baltimore Colts that started in 1953, then moved to Indianapolis in 1984. Nor should they be confused with the Baltimore Ravens who were originally the Cleveland Browns (who replaced the Cleveland Rams, who later moved to LA), then moved to Baltimore in 1996. The Cleveland Browns, who moved to Baltimore, *should be* confused with the Cleveland Browns mentioned above, because they are them. If you understand all of the above, read it again.

CLEVELAND BROWNS

FOUNDED 1944

In an act of egotism akin to people naming their kids after themselves and the Gap naming their children's store "Baby Gap," the Cleveland Browns are named after their original coach and cofounder, Paul Brown. They got lucky. What if Paul's surname was "Lipshitz" or "Buttcheeks"? Just ask the AA baseball Norfolk Assmanowitzes how they feel.

The Browns' official colors are brown and orange, a tribute to Cleveland's famous sewage, and they're the only team still without a logo on their helmets.

CLEVELAND BROWNS

Their logo used to be one of those hardware store paint strips that showed various shades of brown, but the team knew they needed a change when married couples left games arguing about what color would look best in the den.

In the AAFC, the Browns dominated, winning the championship every season. After joining the NFL, they went on to win championships in 1950, '54, '55, and '64, and then . . . stopped. We now know they were saving their strength for something even more exhausting than an NFL championship season: moving. In 1996, owner Art Modell moved the team to Baltimore. Cleveland kept the name "Browns" and any rolls of packing tape left behind.

The Browns got a new team in 1999 but have since only had three winning seasons, just two playoff appearances, and only one playoff win. In 2017, they became the second franchise (after the Lions) to have an 0-16 season. Currently, the only thing they aren't losing is money on victory champagne.

NOTABLE BROWNS

MARION MOTLEY–In the 1940s and '50s, he averaged an amazing 5.7 yards per carry. If we ignore Fritz Pollard and Bobby Marshall, as history often does, Motley was also one of the first two African Americans to break the color barrier (with Bill Willis) in 1946.

JIM BROWN–One of the greatest players in NFL history, he went to the Pro Bowl every year he played and is the only player to average more than 100 rushing yards per game for his career. In retirement, he became an actor, once guest starring on the TV show *CHiPs* as a pickpocket on roller skates. He is also considered one of the greatest NFL players ever to portray a pickpocket on roller skates.

OZZIE NEWSOME–In retirement, he was the general manager of the Ravens, the first African American to hold that position in the NFL. As a player, he was a three-time Pro Bowler.

NOTE: Newsome was not an actual *professional bowler*, although, if he dedicated himself, he could be. Ozzie, if you're reading this, you're a great athlete, and Cleveland is hosting the PWBA Bowlers Journal Open. What are you waiting for?

SAN FRANCISCO 49ERS

FOUNDED 1946

The first major sports franchise in San Francisco, they've won five Super Bowls and in 2022 were ranked the twelfth most valuable sports team in the world, well ahead of the Topeka Central High School Chess Club.

NOTABLE 49ERS

JOE MONTANA–One of the all-time greats, he won four Super Bowls and, in 2006, was rated the number-one clutch quarterback of all time by *Sports Illustrated*. *Sports Illustrated* was a magazine. Magazines were things people bought at newsstands. Newsstands were places where people could buy magazines, like, for example, *Sports Illustrated*.

JERRY RICE–A three-time Super Bowl champion and thirteen-time Pro Bowler, he is widely considered the greatest receiver of all time. From Joe Montana passes to cabs at rush hour, there was nothing he couldn't catch.

RONNIE LOTT–A four-time Super Bowl champion, he had seven interceptions in his 1981 rookie season and finished second in "Rookie of the Year" to Lawrence Taylor, which is like finishing second to Mount Everest in the "Tallest Mountain" competition.

INDIANAPOLIS COLTS

FOUNDED 1946

(as the Miami Seahawks)

The Seahawks moved to Baltimore in 1947, changed their name to the Colts, and were disbanded in 1950. They were revived in 1953 and went on to win three NFL Championships and one Super Bowl. In 1984, owner Robert Irsay infamously packed up in the middle of the night and moved the team to Indianapolis. Irsay was upset the city of Baltimore wouldn't pay for stadium improvements (though hiring movers to work in the middle of the night couldn't have been cheap either). Despite the team's success in Indianapolis, it's almost as if a ghostly spirit wants the team to return to its original home, since every Super Bowl the Colts franchise has ever played in has been in Miami. This odd fact may bore you, win you a trivia contest, or both.

NOTABLE COLTS

JOHNNY UNITAS—Led the Colts to three NFL Championships and one Super Bowl. Between 1956 and 1960, he had forty-seven consecutive games throwing a TD, a record that lasted fifty-two years, until 2012, when Drew Brees went fifty-four. But the peak of Unitas's stellar career came when, on the TV show *The Simpsons*, a character said, "Now, Johnny Unitas, there's a haircut you could set your watch to."

JOHN MACKEY—Only the second tight end to be inducted into the Hall of Fame, he was also the first president of the National Football League Players Association. Originally formed as a way for players to get discounts on car insurance and dry cleaning, this union surprisingly proved helpful in improving salaries and safety.

MARVIN HARRISON—A Super Bowl champ and eight-time All-Pro, he played his entire career for Indianapolis mostly because he had a great parking spot and didn't want to give it up. To be fair, it was right near the players' entrance, in the shade, and ranked one of the top 100 parking spots of all time.

INDIANAPOLIS COLTS

PEYTON MANNING—Part of the Manning dynasty, he won a Super Bowl for Indianapolis and then another playing for Denver, becoming the first QB to win Super Bowls in different cities. Manning often called audibles at the line of scrimmage and was thus nicknamed "The Sheriff." This is because in the Wild West, lawmen would have a detailed plan for how to confront a gang of outlaws, but then, as the outlaws patiently waited, the sheriff would change everything, usually by repeatedly yelling "Omaha."

PAT MCAFEE—"Punter, sportscaster, YouTube star, and pro wrestler" is both a summary of his career and also what inmates at mental asylums put on their résumés as they prep for the big career fair. McAfee is undoubtedly entertaining, a term not usually ascribed to punters or punting.

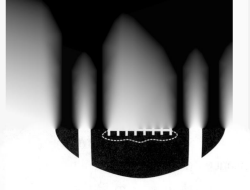

Punters

You see them come on the field and think, *Hey, now's my chance to go to the bathroom!* but punters are as integral to the game as that towel hanging from the linesman's belt or those sleeveless parkas they drape over cold quarterbacks.

The best punts land in the "coffin corner," where the sideline meets the end zone. This term originated in 1982 when Dolphins brass agreed to bury die-hard fans at this spot on the field. It was a wonderful final place of rest for many until a poorly secured coffin lid and a very muddy field led to a cadaver's hand making a touchdown-saving tackle. The deceased's widow was subsequently moved to the players' wives' and girlfriends' section of the stands since her husband was the Dolphins' leading tackler that day.

The Shortest Punt Ever

Negative seven yards, kicked by the Giants' Sean Landeta (1985)

It started with Landeta missing the snap and the ball bouncing around him. Luckily, someone jumped on the loose ball. Unluckily, it was an opponent on the Chicago Bears. Luckily, the Bears only ran the ball back five yards. Unluckily, after those five yards they were in the end zone. So, bad luck, good luck, everything evened out. Except the score—the Bears won 21–0.

The Longest Punt Ever

Ninety-eight yards, kicked by the Jets' Steve O'Neal (1969)

The ball, kicked from the Jets' own end zone into Denver's thin air, flew seventy-five yards, over the returner, and bounced to the Broncos' one yard line for a total of ninety-eight yards. When O'Neal's overjoyed teammates lifted him in the air, O'Neal traveled forty-three yards, setting the record for longest punter tossing.

Who's Who on an NFL Sideline

BRIAN KELLEY

An NFL team is a complicated machine, never more so than on game day. These are some of the lesser-known coaches, assistants, and other team employees whose tireless work on the sidelines keeps your favorite team playing its best!

Stunt Coordinator

Whenever a play design calls for physical contact between athletes, the stunt coordinator works with the NFL's talented community of stuntmen to ensure that the on-field action looks as realistic as possible.

Offensive Linebackers Coach

Offensive linebacker is not currently a position under NFL rules, but teams want to be ready should things change. Phil Brodski, the current offensive linebackers coach for the Dallas Cowboys, has forty-three years of NFL service. He spends months on the road, scouting the college ranks for athletes with the special blend of speed and power necessary, he's guessing, to play offensive linebacker at the highest level. At the practice facility, Coach Brodski runs his players through drills, teaching them how to tackle players on their own team.

"Near as I can figure," explains Brodski, "that's what an offensive linebacker would do. But I could be way off. Hopefully we never have to find out, because if they ever activate my guys, it's going to ruin football."

Ryan Fitzpatrick

Under the latest collective bargaining agreement, Ryan Fitzpatrick is available to all thirty-two teams should their starting quarterback get injured, even though Ryan

Fitzpatrick has "retired." Ryan Fitzpatrick comes with substantial risks, which you should carefully consider before activating Ryan Fitzpatrick. If you choose to proceed, flip a coin. If it's heads, Ryan Fitzpatrick throws for six hundred yards and twelve touchdowns. Tails, and Ryan Fitzpatrick throws twenty interceptions.

Either way, you must now sign Ryan Fitzpatrick to a one-year, $15 million contract after the game. Be advised that your fan base, for some reason, now loves Ryan Fitzpatrick more than the twenty-one-year-old rookie you drafted at number one overall. Be further advised that this rookie, the reigning Heisman Trophy winner, will never play football again. He will spend the rest of his days hearing the ghostly footsteps of Ryan Fitzpatrick sneaking up to steal his job. Trade him for a future seventh-round pick.

Next, rewrite your entire playbook around Ryan Fitzpatrick, then watch hopelessly as every play, even the running plays, ends with Ryan Fitzpatrick screaming "Let's f-ing go!" as he hurls the ball as far as he can downfield. At the end of the season, move on from Ryan Fitzpatrick. But also know, deep down, that there is no moving on from Ryan Fitzpatrick, and that he carries a piece of your soul forever tucked away inside his beard.

Sideline Sketch Artist

In recent years, a growing number of NFL executives have voiced concern that the presence of television cameras at games has a sensationalizing effect on the proceedings. "I was at the NFC Championship Game a few years back, and it was a media circus," lamented one current team president. "Everyone screaming at the tops of their lungs, players knocking each other over just to get to the ball. I stared at the chaos, thinking, *I don't know what this is, but it isn't football.*"

In response, several NFL cities have banned cameras from their stadiums. Instead, sketch artists are employed to capture key moments of the game so that fans can experience them in the next day's newspaper. This explains why you've never seen, or probably even heard of, teams like the Salt Lake City Wranglers, the Syracuse Blitz, or the Jacksonville Jaguars.

Microsoft Surface Technician

In 2013, Microsoft signed an exclusive contract with the NFL requiring all teams to use the company's Surface tablet during games. Since then, a highly trained Microsoft engineer is posted on each team's sideline to make sure that the cases reading "Microsoft Surface" don't slip off the iPads inside.

Team Jester

Clad in motley of the most delightful hues, the jester prances the sidelines astride his hobby horse. Bells merrily a-jingling, he dispenses cutting barbs and bawdy rhymes that help players and coaches not take themselves too seriously. Often, he is the only member of the staff who can deliver bad news to the head coach. After Super Bowl 20, it was longtime Patriots fool Fumblin' Tom who informed Head Coach Raymond Berry that his team had suffered a humiliating 46–10 loss. "You put up a valiant fight," he quipped, "unlike your players, who got creamed!"

Lip Reader

Using high-powered binoculars, the Lip Reader spies on the opposing team's coaches, stealing plays as they are sent in. "It's a waiting game," says Pete Zweibak, Lip Reader for the Washington Commanders. "Patience is the hunter's deadliest weapon, and I am nothing if not patient."

Zweibak trains his glasses on the other team's offensive coordinator. The OC studies his play sheet, selects a play, and activates the headset connection to his quarterback. "Yes, my sweet . . ." says Zweibak, relishing the moment of the kill. "No one's watching. It's perfectly safe. Tell me . . . *everything.*" Suddenly, Zweibak recoils in horror. "He's covering his mouth with the edge of the play sheet! I . . . I can't see his lips! What spectacular cunning is this! It's like he knows lip reading is a thing, but–but that's impossible!"

Backup Quarterback

Casual fans might look down on these guys as "clipboard holders," but they're an integral part of their team's success. Backup QBs have to stay mentally and physically prepared to play at a moment's notice, despite receiving few reps in practice. On game day, they assist the coaching staff, analyzing defensive schemes and devising adjustments. That's why many career backups, like Doug Pederson, Frank Reich, and Gary Kubiak, go on to become successful NFL head coaches.

Third-String Quarterback

Realistically, is this guy ever going to play? No way! Not under *this* coaching staff, which wouldn't recognize arm talent if it hit them in the numbers from seventy yards. Which is *exactly* the throw the third-string QB made in practice that one time. Remember *that* toss? But, of course, the coaches were too busy fawning all over the starter to notice. So, what's the point? The *second* the head coach's back is turned, the third-string QB is gonna drop his clipboard, crack open a beer, and fire up some of his "signature brats" on the grill he stashed behind the medical tent.

Fourth-String Quarterback

He's the guy in the flip-flops and shirt that reads "KEG STAND CHAMPION." When he's sober enough to speak, which is rare, the fourth-stringer will tell anyone in earshot that this whole sideline party is a real "sausage fest," but that's all gonna change once the frat makes him Social Chairman.

Fifth-String Quarterback

Spends the game floating face down in a tank of Fireball Cinnamon Whisky.

Sixth-String Quarterback

An undrafted free agent from a Division III school in Wisconsin, this go-getter keeps his head in the game, listens in on player-coach discussions, and works tirelessly to hone his craft. Get a load of the next Tom Brady over here! After the game, we're all gonna kick his ass. Who's in?

THE
1950s

BIG LEAGUE ON CAMPUS

DAN This is that time when the NFL grew out of its awkward stage, started dating television, and suddenly became popular. With the absorption of players from AAFC teams, the quality of play went up, and soon NFL games were being watched by more viewers than even the *Perry Mason* episode "The Case of the Restless Redhead" (the one where, at the end, Evelyn is cleared of all charges).

1951

The Rams' Norm Van Brocklin has a 554-yard passing day. This record still stands, although many, like the Bengals' Joe Burrow, are getting close (525 in 2021). One great day, great player, or game against the Lions, and this record could be broken.

1953/54

Joe Perry of the 49ers becomes the first back-to-back 1,000-yard rusher. Perry was also the first African American to be NFL MVP. He retired in 1963 as the league's all-time rushing yards leader, but his number 34 jersey continued to play for fourteen more years until it was retired by the 49ers.

1959

The Packers hire Vince Lombardi, a Giants assistant, as their coach. Lombardi would go on to compile a 98-30-4 record and win five NFL Championships and the first two Super Bowls. The Super Bowl Trophy is now called the Lombardi Trophy, presumably after him.

DAN Speaking of Vince Lombardi, why is the Lombardi Trophy a metal football? The Stanley Cup isn't shaped like a hockey puck. The World Series trophy isn't shaped like a baseball. Yes, we're conveniently forgetting about the NBA's Larry O'Brien Trophy (just like the Denver Nuggets have since they were founded).

Is it so the metal football can serve as a backup in case they run out of regular footballs? If that happens, how does Tom Brady deflate a metal football?

Speaking of Tom Brady, after the Buccaneers' 2021 Super Bowl win, Brady *did* actually throw the trophy from a boat on which he was celebrating to TE Cameron Brate, who was celebrating on a different boat. But due to the trophy's shape, Brady had to dump it off with a sort of awkward lateral—even though there wasn't a pass rusher within miles. So, whoever designed this trophy for slightly drunk quarterbacks to throw in a tight spiral from boat to boat, you failed. You're forgiven, but try to do better next time.

★★★ HISTORICAL HISTORY ★★★

1958—The Best Game Ever Played

No, not Jenga—that year's championship game between the Colts and Giants. As much as the NFL was gaining attention, this game really put it over the top, just like what happened with M&M's when they came out with the pretzel one. It's called "The Greatest Game Ever Played," featured twelve Hall of Famers, and was the first NFL game to go to overtime. It's estimated that 45 million people watched on television, which is roughly 45 million more than will ever read this book.

The Worst Game Ever?

A game as great as that 1958 matchup between the Colts and Giants begs the question: What's the *worst* game ever played? Quit begging, because here's the answer.

Internet consensus points to November 4, 1979, when the Seahawks lost to the Rams 24–0, with Seattle totaling –7 yards for the game. That's *negative* yards, the golf equivalent of hitting your tee shot off your golf cart and killing your caddy.

On top of the low-quality play on the field, the concessions guys had mistakenly switched the ketchup and mustard in the pump containers, every beer vendor had what doctors call "chemical warfare body odor," and a grizzly bear was loose in section RR, mistaking red-faced, embarrassed Seattle fans for salmon. It was, by all accounts, a bad game.

94

NEW ENGLAND PATRIOTS

FOUNDED 1959

(as the Boston Patriots)

They started in the AFL but joined the NFL in 1970 and then, upon moving to Foxborough in 1971, changed their name to the New England Patriots. Along with Pittsburgh, they share the record for most Super Bowl wins (six). Like any impressive dynasty, the Patriots have also enjoyed their share of scandals: Deflategate, Spygate, the Iran-Contra Affair, and the sinking of the RMS *Lusitania*.

NOTABLE PATRIOTS

TOM BRADY—The most famous football player in the world, he has success, looks, money . . . yet there's one thing Tom will never have. When players were lined up alphabetically for field trips, he was behind Keenan Allen every time. And he always will be. That's something Brady has to live with every day. Every. Single. Day.

JOHN HANNAH—Considered one of the greatest offensive linemen of all time. He foolishly played for the Patriots when they sucked and consequently never won a Super Bowl. If he could have just held on for seventeen more years, the guy would have a ring.

ROB GRONKOWSKI—"Gronk" played nine years for the Patriots, then two for the Buccaneers, winning four Super Bowls. A great tight end, the 6'6", 265-pound dynamo bursts with joy on and off the field, sort of like if Frankenstein's monster was on Zoloft.

BILL BELICHICK—Coached eight Super Bowl winners and is first all-time in playoff coaching wins. He's also set many records for surliness and short answers at press conferences that will never be beaten.

Meet "Pat Patriot"

Today, the Patriots' logo is a sleek silver-surfer head, but for a long time, the logo was a Continental Army soldier snapping a football. With great time and expense, we tracked down Steve Gould, the man who posed for that image. The following is a transcript of our phone interview with Gould.

In 1960, you were a Revolutionary War reenactor, correct?

Yeah, that's right. During the week, I had my air-conditioning repair gig, but on weekends, I was out there, re-creating the battle of Lexington and Concord. I don't want to brag, but I was probably the best to ever do it. I mean, I was always on the winning side. How many guys spend their careers undefeated? Not many. Maybe me and nobody. That's who.

And one day you were asked to pose for the New England Patriots helmet?

Yeah, some guy asks if I can bring my outfit to this place in the city. I tell him it's stupid. I mean, who ever heard of a patriot, in full dress, snapping a football? But for two hundred dollars, I shut up fast. Hell, dry cleaning those tricorn hats ain't cheap. So yeah, that's me on the helmet. I'm kind of the Jerry West of football, but more like the Jerry Northeast—get it? 'Cause I'm a patriot? Don't worry, no one ever gets it.

You were the logo for thirty-two years.

Yup. And then, no call, no nothing, they switch to something called "The Flying Elvis." I was angry. I got bitter. I did some things I'm not proud of, like auditioning for the Raiders' pirate and the Viking guy and even, in a real low moment, the Atlanta Falcon. I was hurting. A lot. Still am. (pauses) I gotta go. (hangs up)

KANSAS CITY CHIEFS

FOUNDED 1959

(as the Dallas Texans) (AFL)

Lamar Hunt's team when he founded the AFL, in 1963 they moved to Kansas City, and bending to logic and geography, renamed themselves the Chiefs. Seven years later, they joined the NFL in the 1970 merger and have since won three Super Bowls. Like Washington, the Chiefs have also faced criticism for their name and appropriation of Indigenous American culture, but they have bravely or stupidly (isn't most bravery just stupidity?) not made any significant changes as of yet.

NOTABLE CHIEFS

TONY GONZALEZ—He played 270 games and lost only two fumbles on 1,327 touches. He wasn't as sure-handed in his personal life, though, and has, according to the Elias Sports Bureau, misplaced his car keys 36 times on just 831 touches. They're usually on his dresser but have also been in his pockets, leading to them once going into the washing machine, requiring new batteries in the fob.

PAT MAHOMES—The only quarterback in history to throw for more than 5,000 yards in a season in both college and the NFL. He and Peyton Manning are the only players in history to throw 50 touchdown passes and 5,000 yards in a season. Mahomes has also led the Chiefs to two Super Bowl wins. In both games, he was voted MVP, joining Tom Brady and Joe Montana as one of the only quarterbacks to be MVP of both the regular season and Super Bowl multiple times. All this success has let Mahomes realize his childhood dream: becoming the star of some insurance commercials.

TRAVIS KELCE—He holds the NFL records for most consecutive seasons with 1,000 yards receiving by a tight end (seven) and most receiving yards by a tight end in a single season (1,416). If Kelce retired right now, he'd surely be in the Hall of Fame, but if he keeps playing, he can make a ton of money and then be in the Hall of Fame. After a few seconds of thought, he's chosen the second option.

NEW YORK JETS

FOUNDED 1959

(as the New York Titans)

Why even talk about the Jets when the next chapter's all about them? But listen, if you're a Jets fan, just assume the book ends here and ignore anything after this. Trust us, it's all legal disclaimers and that garbage where the writers thank their stupid families. So, end of book. Thanks for reading. Bye!

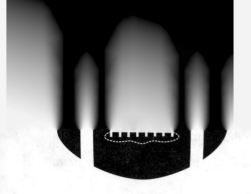

In a Changing World, There's One Constant: The Jets Stink

Every day, the sun rises and sets, we wake and we sleep, and the New York Jets stink, suck, blow, and anything else you'd expect from a broken vacuum.

The Jets are bad. Historically bad. New York Jets–level bad. They were lousy even from their 1959 beginning as the New York Titans. Why the Titans? Because New York already had the Giants, and the team founders reasoned, "Titans are bigger than Giants."

The team had just been formed and already it was relying on flawed logic. The size a thing is named after has no correlation to its success. Look at the triumph of Apple and the failure of Sun Microsystems (if not familiar with either, the sun is bigger than most apples). Lions are big but Detroit gets regularly trounced by puny things like Seahawks, Cardinals, and whatever a "Charger" is.

The Titans hovered around .500 their first three seasons, and by 1962 bordered on bankruptcy—financially and, presumably, morally. In '63, they were sold and changed their name to the New York Jets, choosing that name because they'd soon be moving to play near La Guardia Airport, a trainwreck that consistently ranks as "Worst Airport in the U.S." Therefore, choosing "Jets" was like naming your kid off a movie playing on the maternity ward TV and leaving with a bouncing baby "Leatherface."

DAN A quick apology to all Leatherface fans reading this. We know he's "your guy."

They also chose "Jets" because it rhymes with "Mets," the team they'd be sharing Shea Stadium with. But like La Guardia or eyebrow dandruff, the Mets also aren't something with which you want to be affiliated. In fact, the year before the Jets chose their name, the Mets lost 120 games, the most ever in a modern MLB season.

As long as we're insulting New York landmarks, Shea Stadium (may it rest in peace) also sucked. It was an eyesore, and an earsore, because it constantly had planes overhead—because it was *right next to La Guardia Airport!* The worst airport! Planes couldn't fly away fast enough. Just think how many Jets audibles were bungled because no one could hear with Delta flight 1438 passing overhead.

Choosing the name "Jets" was a hat trick of bad decisions (almost as bad as using a hockey term to talk about football). Once crowned the Jets, the team rose from the Titans' ashes of failure to find . . . even more failure. Their next three seasons all had records of 5–8–1. Pity the quality, admire the consistency.

DAN Hold on a minute. The Jets haven't always been bad. They did win the Super Bowl in 1969. Ask around—you'll see I'm right.

Yes, that's true. The Jets did win the 1969 Super Bowl. It's acknowledged, but only because it happened. After six straight years of garbage, the Jets drafted a handsome, dimple-chinned quarterback named Joe Namath who was also, fortunately, very good at football. With Namath under center, the Jets won it all.

To the outside world, this seemed like something to celebrate, but for the Jets organization, it was when they hit rock bottom. This was a franchise dedicated to defeat, and they'd just ruined all that. They could've been the best at being the worst, but now, they'd even failed at failure. This was their Chernobyl.

NOTE: In 1969, Chernobyl hadn't happened yet. When it did, the Soviets described it as their "форсунки супер чаша" (Jets Super Bowl).

That unfortunate championship led to some serious soul-searching for the Jets. Chairs were pulled into circles so people could "really talk." There were off-site bonding getaways and trust exercises. It wasn't easy. Nothing important ever is. But it worked. The Jets rediscovered their purpose and settled back into their rut. Since then, they've avoided another Super Bowl, and as of the end of the 2022 season, they have an all-time record of 421–537–8—a legacy of losing they can be proud of.

Analyzing Jets Fans Using the Wong–Baker FACES Pain Rating Scale

0	2	4	6	8	10
Gambler who bets on any team playing the Jets. As a result, very wealthy.	Either not a Jets fan or a Jets fan but heavily medicated.	Bar owner where Jets fans drown sorrows. Conflicted, but also wealthy.	New season ticket holder realizing team is bad, first quarter of the first game.	Parent finding Jets jersey in kid's closet. Debating giving kid up for adoption.	First-rounder just picked by Jets. Debating retirement.

When you lose so often, it's natural for fans to turn to some sort of crutch—drink, prayer . . . drunk prayer? Searching for answers, some Jets fans assume that, like with eclipses, the only possible explanation is the occult. Hence, they believe the Jets are cursed. Even a respected expert like Wikipedia says: *Legend has it that the reason the Jets won the Super Bowl is because Joe Namath made a deal with the Devil—if the Jets won that game, they would never have to win anything ever again.*

This theory falls apart for two reasons:

1. The Devil wouldn't have the patience to oversee the Jets post-curse. He'd get frustrated with all the stupid penalties and missed opportunities, and end up switching to a better game or a reality show he created like *The Real Housewives of Potomac*.
2. The Devil is represented by super-agent Drew Rosenhaus, and there's no way Rosenhaus would let his client make a deal this long. Maybe a two-year deal with options, at most.

So no, the Jets aren't cursed. They're merely the result of a bad beginning, bad karma, and bad decisions, with bad luck piled on top—the exact recipe for Olive Garden lasagna!

The proof isn't just the Jets' win–loss record (loss–loss record?). It's also evident in the team's frequent scandals and screwups, such as:

1983: Draft-Aster

The Jets could've drafted QB Dan Marino but instead chose QB Ken O'Brien. Dan Marino is in the Hall of Fame. Ken O'Brien isn't even in the Hall of Fine.

1995: Draft-Aster 2: This Time, It's Personnel

The Jets could've chosen Warren Sapp, who went on to become a Hall of Famer. They picked Kyle Brady, who went on to become a licensed financial advisor.

Draft-Asters 3–300

Footballoutsiders.com (a website—you can tell from the ".com") studied NFL teams' "draft return" in 2020—and guess who finished last? The Jets. The *New York Post* (a newspaper, though aren't papers now pretty much just websites?) analyzed each team's draft history over the previous five years and the Jets finished twenty-third. These bad drafts are even worse when you realize the Jets always pick early because they stink up the regular season; they still find the turds hidden in the pile of diamonds. The Jets choose players like hyenas choose which antelope to attack: the weak, the injured, the future licensed financial advisors.

The Belichick Era: January 3, 2000–January 4, 2000

Bill Belichick was hired as the Jets' coach. Fans were excited, the team's tailors started cutting sleeves off sweatshirts, and then, the very next day, Belichick quit. After just one day. That's something angry teenage fast-food workers do. Also like an angry teenage fast-food worker, Belichick wrote his resignation on a napkin. History is unclear if he also pumped ketchup on his name tag before storming out to wait for his mom to pick him up, but probably.

Twenty-three days later, Belichick became the coach of the Patriots. He now has more Super Bowl rings than sour expressions. Having mellowed with age, nowadays the only thing Coach Belichick uses napkins for is to wipe his mouth or to prop up a camera illegally hidden to tape an opposing team's practice (see "The New England Patriots, dirty, filthy cheaters"). By the way, the team Belichick illegally taped? The Jets!

DAN Great learning opportunity here and further proof that nothing good comes out of illegally filming your ex.

2003: Namath Goes 0 for 1

Joe Namath, the QB that briefly, accidentally made the Jets good, was interviewed while drunk on the sidelines and chose to answer the reporter's question with "I want to kiss you. I could care less about the team struggling." This would have been a great answer if the reporter had asked, "Joe, what's the most inappropriate thing you can say right now?" Sadly, that wasn't the question.

2012: The "Butt Fumble"

In the playoff hunt, while facing the Patriots, Jets QB Mark Sanchez ran into his own lineman's butt, the ball popped loose, and the Pats ran it back for six. It was shameful and tragic. President Barack Obama sent FEMA to New York, declaring the team a national disaster. The rest of the world took notice, too. The Hague declared, "We wouldn't wish this on even our worst enemy. Well, maybe Russia."

Following the Butt Fumble, artists worldwide tried to capture the anguish. Some examples:

"お尻のファンブル"– haiku by Momoko Kuroda, Japan

Seasons pass like ships
Jets stay still, rust, rot, mildew
And hope dies lonely

A limerick by Algernon Charles Swinburne, Ireland

Mark Sanchez was a proud New York Jet
Who fumbled when ball and butt met
Thus making league history
And solving the mystery
Of how pathetic the sad Jets could get

"Ballad of the Butt Fumble"—song by Gordon Lightfoot, Canada

Son, that was an awful day
When underneath a sky of grey
We watched a butt give a game away.
Remember it like yesterday
And still feel cold, full of dismay.

The Jets were hanging in, all was in order
'Til early on in the second quarter.
Sanchez scrambled to make a play
His lineman's butt got in his way.
The ball popped loose, off that caboose,
The Pats ran it back for a score.
Playoff chances out the door
Playoff chances out–

DAN Wait, stop the song. Yes, it's a touching ballad that would be great for the father-daughter dance at any wedding, but making fun of the Jets feels wrong. It's just too easy, kicking a team when they're down.

Actually, we brought in Jets kicker Doug Brien to kick the team when they're down. Sadly, he missed and clunked them off the cross bar.

DAN I'm 80 percent sure that didn't happen. Anyway, people and bumper stickers often say, "If you're not part of the solution, you're part of the problem." So, how about we try and offer some answers?

Fair enough. Here, therefore, is a plan to make the Jets good (a topic that's never come up at a Spirit Airlines meeting):

FIVE-STEP PLAN TO FIX THE JETS

1. Move the team to Portland. Why? Well, as the Jets have taught us, a team's success is tied to the airport they play near, and Portland's airport is constantly ranked quite high.

2. On draft day, management needs to remember the simple mantra: "Your every thought is incompetent" (YETII). Instead of thinking, they should rely on websites, or rankings, or just watch live coverage where analysts talk about who the next obvious pick is and then do that.

3. Don't let any coaches near napkins. In fact, don't even have napkins in the building—they're too easy to resign on! For the same reason, no pens, paper, computers, Wi-Fi—not even any talking allowed in the office. If a future Hall of Fame coach wants to quit, they're gonna have to do it via hula.

4. Tell the players, "Please don't run the ball into other players' butts." Maybe even get some signs made and put them up everywhere.

5. Change the team's name to the "Patriots." This alone won't make the team better, but in games where the Patriots are crushing the former Jets, if both teams have the same name, there's a chance the scorer will give the former Jets some points by accident. Yes, part of this strategy is rooting for "clerical error."

With this simple plan, the Portland Patriots will be a championship team New York can be proud of. Or at least, not an embarrassment. P-A-T-R-I-O-T-S! Patriots! Patriots! Patriots!

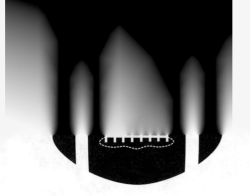

Football and TV, a Match Made in Money

DAN Since the "Greatest Game Ever Played" connected with viewers in 1958, football has become the United States' most-viewed TV product of all time. Elections, celebrity trials, and horrific news stories only wish they were football. The NFL currently has TV deals in place through the 2033 season estimated to be worth more than $100 billion. Today, games are shown on Mondays, Thursdays, Saturdays, and even—occasionally—Sundays.

Some moments in football broadcast history:

1939—The first televised NFL game, on October 22.

1955—The first football game (a college game) covered by the Goodyear Blimp. Blimps still provide aerial shots today, even when games are indoors. This sounds useless, but it's helpful for letting stadium owners know if they have leaves in their gutters or a Frisbee on their roof.

1970—Monday Night Football begins broadcasting with a Jets versus Browns game, with Howard Cosell, Don Meredith, and Keith Jackson in the booth. Monday night games not only showed football when more people were home, but it also gave gamblers a chance to win back the money they lost on Sunday (they often didn't).

1986—Instant replay becomes a part of the game. Also, in 1986, instant replay becomes a part of the game.

1987—The first game on ESPN and also consequently the first game shown on cable TV.

2015—Yahoo hosts the first global livestream of a regular season game. More than 15.2 million viewers watch while ignoring banner ads to "reconnect with old classmates."

Broadcasters have also made many technical advances to enhance the viewing experience over the years. Things like:

The First Down Line

In this era of phone apps that teach you how to swear in Portuguese, NFL refs still measure first downs with the caveman technology of two orange sticks connected by a ten-yard chain. Many of these same officials have also spurned the score clock and instead prefer using sundials. This has proven to be a real problem in domed stadiums.

Luckily, television invented an answer: a yellow line projected onto our screens so we can see where players need to get to for a first down. So why aren't officials using it? And also, why aren't players? If players could see the distance needed, never again would a receiver run a route on third down that's too short. The only possible downsides of a laser beaming across the field are that it may get blocked by an obstruction and/or it could possibly make everyone sterile. Still, those are risks we viewers are willing to take.

The Field Goal Line

Like the first down line, broadcasts show viewers where teams need to be to kick a field goal. This "field goal" line has a lot of assumptions behind it: Did they account for the wind? The leg strength of the kicker? The kicker's mental state, horoscope, and mother's maiden name? It's also fair to assume a ball will travel farther in air with a high concentration of belches in it, so do they move the line in stadiums full of gassy fans (like Cincinnati)? If all of this *isn't* incorporated, the technology is useless and should be moved to the concourse to tell thirsty fans how far from the beer stand they can be to get a cold one and still make it back to their seats before the second half begins.

The Red Zone Channel

Existing solely on Sundays and jumping from game to game, this channel only shows coverage of teams that are inside their opponents' twenty-yard line. For viewers, this provides a nonstop supply of scoring plays without all the boring, hard work that got the teams there. For bettors or fantasy football players, this is like a nonstop supply of crystal meth shot directly into their eyeballs, without all the boring, hard work of buying the crystal meth, preparing syringes, and so on.

Players Wearing Microphones

The first "mic'd up" player was Pittsburgh linebacker Bill Saul in 1967. Since then, mic'ing up has become a staple of almost every game. Fans mostly hear banal stuff like "Let's go, baby!" and "That's how you do it, baby!" and "Can we hurry this up, my wife is having a baby, baby!" But occasionally, we get to hear what the game sounds like on the field—the grunts, the hits . . . and best of all, the trash talk.

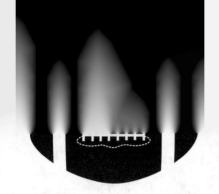

The Best and Worst Trash Talk Ever

The Best Trash Talk

Some players verbally joust at the level of third-grade bullies ("You're ugly" and "Your mom smells weird") but others make mockery an art form. Unlike painting or sculpting, however, good trash talk takes real talent. For example:

"I've eaten burritos bigger than you."
–J. J. Watt (6'5") to Ray Rice (5'9"), 2012

This was either J. J. talking trash or promoting the cookbook he wrote, *10,000 Calories a Day and Each One Yummy*. He famously brings copies to games and tries to sell them to officials during time-outs.

"Is this what you're looking for?"
–Jets cornerback Johnny Sample, Super Bowl 3, 1969
(after intercepting a pass, then holding it up to the intended receiver)

It was a great line and a question Sample himself was asked on a street corner by a guy handing out religious pamphlets and making *way* too much eye contact.

"If that man was on fire and I had to piss to put him out, I wouldn't."

−James Harrison, speaking of commissioner Roger Goodell, 2011

It's worth wondering what scenario would ever put Harrison in this position. Was he playing beer pong while Goodell was nearby doing an inspirational "fire walk" in a flammable polyester jumpsuit? Was Goodell gifting Harrison a hair-trigger flamethrower to celebrate his catheter being removed? We may never know, so let's just enjoy the quote for its poetry.

The Worst Trash Talk

Reprinted here in the interest of giving equal time to the less talented, we also present the following less intimidating on-field chatter:

"We're running it to the left. I just respect you guys
too much to keep secrets from you."

−the Chiefs' Travis Kelce to the Carolina defense, 2020

"Let's do a selfie!"

−Baker Mayfield to Alex Highsmith while Highsmith was sacking him, 2021

Other things overheard, with names withheld to protect the disadvantaged:

"You're overly muscled. Everyone says so!"

"This field is like my dog park and I'm off leash and sniffing asses, baby!"

"Cover me all you want. They never throw to me,
so you're wasting your time."

Microphones have also recorded chitchat in pileups after fumbles:

"Since we're here for a bit, maybe I can walk you through the benefits of a reverse mortgage?"

"Mmm, what is that cologne?"

"Anyone have any tips how to clean a dishwasher? Someone in the last pileup said vinegar works."

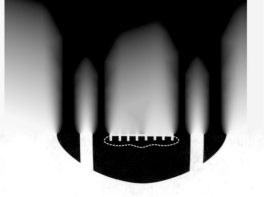

The Media

The magic of TV lets us build relationships with the live broadcasters and media figures that dissect games the rest of the week. When we invite football into our homes, they come along as the game's plus-ones. Some of those greats include:

Jim Nantz—Soft and smart, he's like the smooth jazz of sportscasters. Sometimes you don't even notice him, and he's often on in dentist's offices.

Joe Buck and Troy Aikman—Frequently paired together, they're the perfect combination of knowledge, credibility, square jaws, and coiffed hair. They make a great team. Maybe the greatest team Aikman's ever been on?

Al Michaels and Cris Collinsworth—Michaels, a true legend, famously gave us the classic call "Do you believe in miracles?" and rightfully has a star on the Hollywood Walk of Fame, just in front of the Do You Believe in Miracle Whip Mayonnaise Mega Mart.

Collinsworth was a Pro Bowl Bengals receiver and, once paired with Michaels in the broadcast booth, he originated something called the "Collinsworth Slide." Pre-game, after Michaels welcomed viewers, Collinsworth would slide into frame on his chair. Many hailed this as an iconic act of TV history, but far more have described it as "Huh, I never noticed."

Rich Eisen—He's funny, knowledgeable, and, perhaps even more impressive, runs the forty-yard dash for charity every year at the NFL Scouting Combine (no, we checked; it's actually less impressive). Eisen's best time was 5.94 seconds. Admittedly, that's actually faster than the record slowest time of 6:06, set in 2011 by offensive lineman Isaiah Thompson. Neither Thompson nor Eisen were ever drafted, but at least Thompson has the sense to stop trying to be.

Chris Berman—An early part of ESPN, like so many there he deserves credit for bringing comedy into sportscasting, interlacing highlights with puns and wry comments. Berman famously assigned players clever nicknames, with gems like Joseph "Live and Let" Addai, Jake "Daylight Come and You Gotta" Delhomme, and Mike "You're in Good Hands with" Alstott.

Pat Summerall and John Madden—Summerall, a former player and participant in the "Greatest Game Ever Played," has been called "the quintessential play-by-play voice of the NFL." Madden, the former coach, had passion and a regular-guy persona, and, perhaps more importantly, he popularized the turducken, teaching us it's possible to shove food inside other food. For those who don't know, a turducken is chicken inside a duck inside a turkey. Wow, this has now become a cookbook!

Howard Cosell—A sports icon and the man many of us remember as "the first person we ever hated." He was arrogant and verbose, but undeniably captivating. Cosell hosted the most iconic Monday Night Football trio (with Frank Gifford and Don Meredith) and in that role, broke the news John Lennon had been murdered, establishing both a cultural touchpoint and Cosell's alibi.

Cosell—The Man, The Legend, The Also Other Things

DAN Cosell gave us some of the greatest word salads in broadcasting history. Some were maybe even word paella. Don't believe me? Here are some real things he said and some others he didn't. You, the reader, can guess, in the game . . .

REAL COSELL LINE OR NOT?

1. *Arrogant, pompous, obnoxious, vain, cruel, verbose, a show-off. I have been called all of these. Of course, I am.*

2. *It's not only that I am remarkable at my profession. It's also that all others who attempt it are cursed with limited talent diluted by unlimited blandness.*

3. *Sports is the toy department of human life.*

4. *Will the Beatles ever reunite?*

5. *They brought us this new snack—what do they call them? Nachos?*

6. *Football's a repast requiring eight months to prepare, sixteen weeks to masticate, and as soon as it's fully consumed, we start salivating for a subsequent serving.*

Answer: The false ones are 2 and 6. He said the rest (and with 5 made nachos popular in the United States). He also may have said lines 2 and 6 when no one was listening, in his sleep, or when no one was listening to him sleep.

Dan Patrick—We know him from ESPN, *Football Night in America*, this book, and even as the host of *Sports Jeopardy!*.

Answer: What is a show no one remembers?

Dan Patrick—An Unbiased Examination

Dan is clearly a fixture on the sports landscape, yet discussing him in this book is tricky since it's his name on the cover. How can we represent Dan fairly and objectively? Well, Dan himself had a great idea: Why not include one section in favor of him, and another critical of him? Readers can digest both and decide for themselves. So here we go . . .

IN PRAISE OF DAN PATRICK (unnamed source)

Dan Patrick is a national treasure. No, a global treasure. No, a galactic treasure. He's so omnipresent and omni-awesome that it'd be unfair for any single planet to lay claim to him. The closest analog our simple non-Dan brains can understand is a religious figure, although even religious figures sometimes have flaws and, clearly, Dan has none. He is polished perfection. It's obvious in his work, in the purity and power of his voice, and even more evident when you look at him. Far too much talent has been jam-packed into Mr. Patrick's svelte physique, and his ripped abs are just places where that excess talent is bulging out. Dan, on behalf of all us mere mortals, lacking the gift with words you have, we offer a clumsy, primitive "Thank you for you."

And now, as a rebuttal, a critical view of Dan:

DAN PATRICK, A CRITIQUE (unnamed source)

Have you ever seen a baby bird covered in oil from some horrible offshore spill? Dan has and, unlike you or I, he doesn't just see; he acts. He travels to where Mother Earth is hurting and cleans those birds with the healing waters of his own tears. He summons all his humanity into a tsunami of tenderness and bathes those birds clean. At the same time, somehow, he manages to wash all of us clean, too. His healing powers aren't just reserved for wildlife. His voice is a beacon of hope and joy to everyone who owns a radio, or streams Peacock. While his subject is often sports, that's merely the river this selfless saint travels on, riding a raft made of skill, competence, knowledge, and credibility.

So, there you have it. Two sides of Dan. As with all things, neither of these are probably completely accurate. The truth usually falls somewhere in between.

DAN I accept the results of this fair and objective process. Reading this wasn't easy, but as a professional, I always welcome constructive criticism.

FOOTBALL FUN!

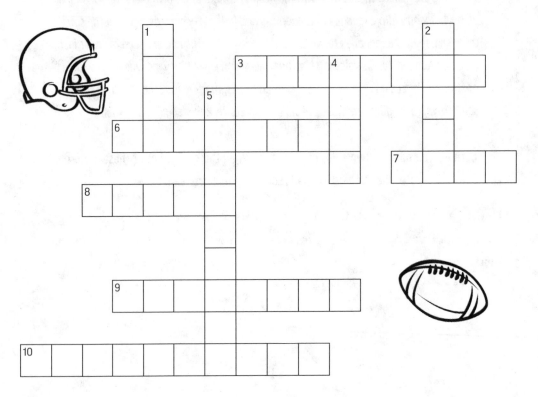

Down:

1. A character who has nothing to do with football (yes, this is a bad hint)
2. Kenny Stabler's nickname and what many owners share DNA with
4. The word "punt." Seriously, just write "punt"
5. Winners of the 2033 Super Bowl (trust us)

Across:

3. A penalty and what the thing on Ryan Fitzpatrick's face needs
6. Calvin Johnson's nickname if he was a Trump supporter
7. A rumored football ream in New York
8. The thing Ryan Fitzpatrick's face is slowly being swallowed by
9. Should be a penalty and what the "Super Bowl Shuffle" was
10. Happens after a TD or when a player changes religion

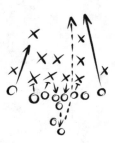

Down: 1. Yoda; 2. snake; 4. punt; 5. Cardinals
Across: 3. clipping; 6. Megatron; 7. Jets; 8. beard; 9. cheap hit; 10. conversion

THE
1960s
PEACE & LOVE & WAR & RIVALRY

DAN The NFL was now firmly at the top of the sports food chain (badminton and tetherball are at the bottom). Then, since it was the 1960s, things got "wild," "far out," and occasionally "radical."

The season expanded to fourteen games, four new teams joined, the Chicago Cardinals moved to St. Louis (probably forever), and in this era of "free love," an illegitimate rival league was born. The father was exactly what you imagine when you think "hippie"—a Texas oilman, Lamar Hunt.

Hunt started the American Football League (AFL) in 1959 after he asked the NFL if he could add a team in Dallas and they said no. That was hurtful enough. Even worse was when the NFL added the Cowboys one year later. Even high school girls at the time described this as "just mean." So, like Elon Musk building his "own girl" after being rejected by a human one, Hunt decided to build his own league.

Hunt chose the acronym "AFL" so it would be first alphabetically if a fan flipped through the phone book looking for a football game they could go to. (Once competitors caught on, the AAFL, AAAFL, and the AAAAFL all launched, then quickly failed.) The AFL was made up of Hunt's Dallas team, teams in Houston, Denver, Los Angeles, New York, and Minneapolis, and eventually Oakland, Boston, and Buffalo. To attract players, they started signing stars right out of college (like Len Dawson and Joe Namath), paying more than they'd make in the NFL. (Life hack: people prefer more money over less money.)

The NFL missed being a monopoly, so in 1966, they made a deal to merge with the AFL. The leagues would play separately, then their champions would meet in "the Super Bowl." In 1970, the two leagues merged entirely, organizing into the American Football Conference (AFC) and the National Football Conference (NFC), and all the rich people involved became even richer, which pleased them.

1960

Detroit drafts Roger Brown, the first 300-pound player. After breaking the weight barrier, Brown goes on to have an exceptional career, playing in six straight Pro Bowls and in the 1962 "Thanksgiving Day Massacre" game, sacking the Packers' Bart Starr *maybe* seven times. It's maybe because NFL records from the game are a little unclear, but what is clear is that as much as the Packers are "massacred," it pales in comparison to what happens to America's turkeys and yams that Thanksgiving.

1960

Red Hickey, the 49ers coach, introduces the shotgun formation. It didn't take off right away, but, with America's love of guns, it was soon widely adopted.

1962

Chuck Bednarik of the Eagles retires. Bednarik was the league's last two-way player for thirty years, until Deion Sanders came along. Hating to see anyone else do something he could do, Bednarik would also spend the time between snaps doing a little officiating and working the scoreboard.

1963

The Football Hall of Fame opens in Canton, Ohio. Why would anyone choose here? (This question is also written below "Welcome to Canton" on signs at the city limits.) The city known as "the Jewel of the Nowhere Belt" was chosen because the NFL was founded at that Hupmobile meeting in Canton, and also because the city is home to the National First Ladies' Library and the league hoped they'd get some visitors who were confused by the NFL/NFLL thing.

1965

Monsanto, the company the world loves for their lethal pesticides and Agent Orange in the Vietnam War, invents "chemgrass." Someone in marketing quickly changes the name to "AstroTurf" and team owners buy it for their stadiums because, like toupees, fake turf doesn't need to be cut and looks good forever. Also like toupees, artificial turf is eventually shown to cause injuries, friction burns, and, in the summer, heat to dangerous levels.

1967

The Packers and Chiefs face off in the first Super Bowl. This also leads to the first-ever Super Bowl party and the consequent first-ever plate of disappointing Super Bowl nachos.

1967

"The Ice Bowl"–This 1967 NFL Championship matchup merits mention in NFL history because . . . the weather is cold. The game's legacy has been protected forever by global climate change.

1969

John Madden takes over as coach of the Raiders. He eventually leads them to a Super Bowl, enjoys a career in broadcasting, and lends his name to a video game franchise that's generated $7 billion and several strained thumb muscles.

TENNESSEE TITANS

★ FOUNDED 1960 ★

(as the Houston Oilers)

The Titans moved to Nashville in 1997, mostly because they're really into country music and those mobile bars that move like a bike when everyone pedals. They're the only team to ever have two players rush for 2,000 yards, with Chris Johnson doing it in 2009 and Derrick Henry in 2020.

NOTABLE TITANS

DERRICK HENRY—Led the league in rushing in 2019 and 2020, when, as noted previously, he also became just the eighth player in history to rush for 2,000 yards. He's nicknamed "King Henry" because of his size and also because he briefly ruled England.

BRUCE MATTHEWS—Over his career, he played every position on the offensive line. Not just versatile, he was also reliable, starting 292 of his 296 career games. This work ethic made him unpopular with lazy people, although they never made the effort to say anything.

EARL CAMPBELL—He was known for his punishing running style and ability to break tackles. A true gentleman, postgame he would pay to replace any tackles he had broken.

WARREN MOON—After going undrafted, he played five seasons in the Canadian Football League, winning five Grey Cups. The Oilers signed him in 1984, and he played another seventeen seasons in the NFL. Moon was the first Black quarterback inducted into the Hall of Fame and the only player in both the NFL and CFL Hall of Fame. His dream of also making the Mexican Pro Football Hall of Fame fell short because no such thing exists.

DENVER BRONCOS

FOUNDED 1960

The Broncos didn't have a winning season their first thirteen years. (At their football bar mitzvah, their speech began "Today I am a team.") They've since won three Super Bowls and play in Empower Field at Mile High Stadium, where one would hope for a lounge called "The Mile High Club," but sadly, sometimes prayers go unanswered.

NOTABLE BRONCOS

JOHN ELWAY–The Colts' first overall pick in the 1983 draft, Elway refused to play for the team and their difficult owner, Robert Irsay, threatening to instead play baseball for the Yankees and their lovable, easygoing owner, George Steinbrenner. The Colts traded him to Denver where he went on to play in five Super Bowls, winning two.

TERRELL DAVIS–The only 2,000-yard rusher to win the Super Bowl the same year. It seems that having a Hall of Fame running back on your team helps your chances to win. Why doesn't every team just do this?

VON MILLER–He's doled out well over 100 career sacks and won a Super Bowl as a Ram (2022) and another with Denver (2016), in which he was also chosen as MVP. He'll be a first ballot Hall of Famer, although with the electoral college, surprises can happen.

JERRY THE KANGAROO–Desperate for quality players, the 1974 Broncos employed a kangaroo as their running back. Jerry scored several touchdowns by hiding the ball in his pouch on long runs but was released after players complained that when the ball came out of the pouch, it was "icky." Jerry now lives with his wife and children in Arizona and is active in real estate.

DALLAS COWBOYS

FOUNDED 1960

They've won five Super Bowls and are the only team to record twenty straight winning seasons (1966 to 1985). They play their games in AT&T Stadium, which, unlike phones on that cell network, always has full bars. According to *Forbes*, they're the most valuable sports team in the world, but since their owner, Jerry Jones, is famously modest, this is a well-kept secret.

NOTABLE COWBOYS

MICHAEL IRVIN—As a receiver, he won three Super Bowls, but in 2009, as a tango-er, he lost on the TV show *Dancing with the Stars*. He blames the loss on letting former Cowboys coach Chan Gailey play-call his dance moves.

TROY AIKMAN—First overall draft pick and three-time Super Bowl champion, he never knew what it felt like to lose. In retirement, he became part owner of the San Diego Padres baseball team, and now he's forgotten what winning is.

TONY DORSETT—Scored ninety-one touchdowns over his career—appropriate, since his initials are TD. In that regard, Tony is envied by his siblings, Virgil Dorsett (VD) and Steven Todd Dorsett (STD).

DEION SANDERS—Played fourteen seasons in the NFL and nine in Major League Baseball. He's the only athlete to play both in a Super Bowl (he won two) and a World Series (he won zero). Not only adept at two sports, when playing football, Sanders played both offense (wide receiver), defense (cornerback), and returned kicks and punts. In a 1996 game against the Bears, he was on the field for almost every play. For all of these amazing athletic feats, Sanders was nicknamed "Prime Time," but research reveals he also performed well in afternoon and morning games.

OAKLAND/LOS ANGELES/OAKLAND/ LAS VEGAS RAIDERS

FOUNDED 1960

They left Oakland and moved to LA from 1982 to 1994, then went back to Oakland in 1995, and to Las Vegas in 2020. We all know that only the most stable people move to Vegas, so this is surely the end of any drama with this franchise.

NOTABLE RAIDERS

GENE UPSHAW—The only player to reach the Super Bowl with the same team in three different decades, something you can only do if you are both great and old.

ART SHELL—A Hall of Fame offensive tackle, he became the second African American head coach in NFL history. He was fired as coach of the Raiders, then, when Al Davis realized he'd have to pay for new business cards for a new coach, rehired again (then fired again one year later).

MARCUS ALLEN—The only player to have won a Heisman, an NCAA Championship, a Super Bowl, NFL MVP, and Super Bowl MVP, and also get a "World's Greatest Father" mug from his kids.

RAY GUY—The first punter ever drafted in the first round, Guy is the only punter in the Hall of Fame. One of his punts once hit a hanging video screen in the Superdome, scaring the opposing team and several pixels.

KENNY STABLER—The "Snake" played hard and partied harder. He was a Super Bowl champ and four-time Pro Bowler, and his five consecutive appearances in conference championship games (1973 to 1977) was a record for quarterbacks for almost forty years, until it was beaten by Tom Brady.

Two Quarterbacks, Two Diets

DAN Kenny Stabler was the Tom Brady of his day—at least in terms of success. In every other way, the two men were complete opposites. The "Snake" and the "No Real Nickname" lived differently, played differently, and, not surprisingly, ate differently. Take a look:

The Tom Brady Diet
Breakfast:
- Avocado
- Eggs from a chicken also following the Tom Brady Diet
- Smoothie (flaxseeds, chia seeds, 1/4 cup of holy water)

NOTE: If you can derive any enjoyment from or taste any flavor in this smoothie, you've made it incorrectly.

Lunch:
- Salad with salmon. The salmon must also have been on the Tom Brady Diet and been a non-smoker.

Dinner:

- Roasted vegetables, which must be on the Tom Brady Diet
- Boiled turkey that has not only been on the Tom Brady Diet, but has also done yoga and meditated regularly

The Kenny Stabler Diet

Breakfast:

- "Breakfast? That's the dinner they serve in the morning, right?"

Lunch:

- Light beer (to brush teeth with)
- Bacon-wrapped cigarette
- Fried oysters, fried chewing tobacco—anything fried, even if it's just the batter
- Three fistfuls bar mix
- One slice processed cheese for a napkin

Dinner:

- One tequila shot for every game lost that season, two for every game won ("You can lick the salt, but don't bite any limes. That's fruit.")
- Whatever you can scavenge from room service trays left in the hotel hallway (**PRO TIP:** Those little bottles of Tabasco sauce make powerful eyedrops.)

- Rice pilaf—not for eating; it's just a good soft thing to pass out in

LOS ANGELES CHARGERS
(NÉE SAN DIEGO CHARGERS)

FOUNDED 1960

Born in LA, they moved to San Diego the next year, then moved back to LA in 2017. They went to their first Super Bowl in 1995, lost, and out of spite have never gone back.

NOTABLE CHARGERS

DAN FOUTS—Fouts led the league in passing for four straight years and became the first player to throw for 4,000 yards in three consecutive seasons. He accomplished all this while also maintaining a luxurious beard that required twenty hours a week of maintenance, including but not limited to grooming, shampooing, and music therapy.

LADAINIAN TOMLINSON—In the 2006 season, he ran in twenty-eight touchdowns, caught three, and even threw for two. It was a season that running backs dream of (along with the standard running back dreams of rocket-powered shoes and a kitten named "Tinker").

KELLEN WINSLOW—He became a legend after a 1982 playoff game against Miami where he had 166 yards receiving, a touchdown, and blocked a field goal. He did all this with a pinched nerve, dehydration, and severe cramps, while needng stitches in his lip. The photo of him being helped off the field by his teammates is an iconic image we couldn't afford to include. Imagine an amazing photo of an amazing player after an amazing game and that's pretty much it.

BUFFALO BILLS

FOUNDED 1960

The Bills are famous for appearing in four straight Super Bowls (1991 to 1994) and losing them all. Bills management, feeling bad, gave all the players "Participant" rings, which now sit lonely in their barren trophy cases.

NOTABLE BILLS

BRUCE SMITH—The NFL all-time sacks leader (200). Any attempt at humor here would take attention away from his incredible career. This restraint and respect will not be repeated.

O. J. SIMPSON—Let's call him "complicated." He was great on the field, still holding the record for single-season yards-per-game average (143.1), but had what some (everyone) would describe as "off-the-field problems." If you're curious what those were, search his name on the internet and then step back as your computer explodes.

JOSH ALLEN—In 2022, he led the Bills to a "perfect game"—every offensive possession ending with a touchdown. "He's the future of the Bills, football, and maybe the world." (This sentence provided by the Bills PR department and approved by The Campaign to Elect Josh Allen President.)

MINNESOTA VIKINGS

FOUNDED 1960

They've made the postseason enough to hold the record for most playoff losses (thirty). As their mother-in-law says, "They're good, but never good enough."

★★★ HISTORICAL HISTORY ★★★

The Worst NFL Play Ever!

There's dispute about this. Was the worst play the Jets' "Butt Fumble"? The "Colts Catastrophe" when they tried to confuse their opponents on a punt by lining up most of their players on one side of the field and instead lost two yards, the ball, self-respect, and eventually the game? Yes, those were horrible, but we're saying the crown for King Loser goes to this one, on October 25, 1964, lovingly called "The Wrong Way Run":

Vikings defensive end Jim Marshall picks up a 49er fumble and runs sixty-six yards to the WRONG end zone. Celebrating, he throws the ball out of bounds, giving the 49ers a safety and all of us a collective moment of thinking, *I'm just glad that wasn't me.*

NOTABLE VIKINGS

RANDY MOSS—He holds records for single-season touchdown receptions (twenty-three) and single-season touchdown receptions for a rookie (seventeen). The term "mossed," meaning "made a leaping catch over a receiver," would be in the NFL dictionary if one existed. Oddly, an *NFL Thesaurus* does exist, as does an *NFL Book of Spells*.

FRAN TARKENTON—When he retired in 1978, he held NFL career records in pass attempts, completions, yardage, touchdowns, QB rushing yards, and wins. Many of those records have since been bested, but that's not his fault; he was fully exonerated by the Minnesota Supreme Court.

ALAN PAGE—During his Hall of Fame career as a defensive tackle, he was also going to law school and eventually became an associate justice of the Minnesota Supreme Court. He wisely recused himself from all dealings on the Fran Tarkenton case referenced above.

ONTERRIO SMITH—This former Viking RB was once stopped at an airport carrying dried urine. Also in his possession was a prosthetic penis called "The Original Whizzinator" that mixed water with dried urine to pass NFL drug tests.

> **DAN** This book does not endorse or denounce the Original Whizzinator, any other products in the Whizzinator family, or the Whizzinator Corporation (of which the authors are stockholders).

ATLANTA FALCONS

FOUNDED 1965

Atlanta was going to join the AFL until the NFL swooped in and offered them a franchise. The Falcons have since been to two Super Bowls, losing both— including in 2017, where they were leading the Patriots 28–3, until they weren't.

NOTABLE FALCONS

JEFF VAN NOTE—A six-time Pro Bowler, he should be in the Hall of Fame but isn't. (Or he is and we didn't research this very well. Both very real possibilities.)

TOMMY NOBIS—A linebacker so respected by his peers that Larry Csonka once said, "I'd rather play against Dick Butkus than Nobis." Nobis was flattered, but Butkus, hearing this, reportedly made a "Whoa, that's a shot!" face.

EUGENE ROBINSON—The day before the Falcons' 1999 Super Bowl, he received the Bart Starr Award for high moral character. That night, he was arrested trying to hire an undercover cop posing as a prostitute. The next day, he lost the Super Bowl. Pointing to the adage "There's no bad publicity," Robinson views the weekend as a major success.

JULIO JONES—A Falcon most of his career, in just 104 games, Jones became the fastest player in NFL history to reach 10,000 total receiving yards. Some sort of math could probably calculate the average receiving yards for each of those games, but isn't it more fun to guess? So let's say ... 23.5 yards per game?

MIAMI DOLPHINS

In 1972, they had the NFL's only perfect season, winning every game, every coin toss, the state lottery, and even two elections for school board trustee. They won the Super Bowl that year, and then, proving it wasn't a fluke, won the next one, too. That last one may have been a fluke, since they haven't won any since and in 2007 had an almost *im*perfect season (1–15), losing almost every game, their phones, and often consciousness. Their logo used to feature a dolphin wearing a helmet and many asked why. The reason: sea mammals take concussions seriously.

In 2013, they changed the logo so the dolphin isn't wearing a helmet. The reason: vanity.

NOTABLE DOLPHINS

DAN MARINO–When he retired, he held every major QB record, including career passing yards and touchdowns. In 1984, he set the record for most yards in a season (5,084) and most touchdown passes (48). Both feats have been outdone now, but if you adjust for inflation, Marino is still on top.

JASON TAYLOR–The best defensive player in Dolphins history, with 139.5 sacks, 46 forced fumbles, and 29 fumble recoveries. He holds the NFL record for most fumbles returned for touchdowns with six. Taylor also returned five fumbles for store credit.

CHANNING CROWDER–A linebacker who played six years with the team and was among the leaders in tackles. He's mentioned here because in an interview he said that he urinated in his pants in the huddle every game. We admire his honesty and his talent, and frown on his poor huddle-training.

NEW ORLEANS SAINTS

FOUNDED 1966

The Saints had twenty consecutive seasons without a winning record. Fans called them the "Aints" and went to games hiding their faces under paper bags. (After several fans fell down the stadium stairs, they realized they should cut out eye holes.) In 2010, the Saints went to their only Super Bowl, won, and have since been reluctant to go to another and risk that perfect record. Home games are played in the Superdome. There's also a Clark Kent Dome in New Orleans but it always seems to disappear whenever the Superdome is around.

NOTABLE SAINTS

DREW BREES—Second in NFL career completion percentage, touchdown passes, passing yards, completions, and pass attempts, Brees also holds the record for consecutive games throwing a touchdown (fifty-four). Early on, his potential was seen as limited because he was only six feet tall. This drove Brees to prove himself with a version of the Napoleon complex doctors dubbed the "Normal Male Height complex."

ALVIN KAMARA—In 2020, he became the second player in history to score six rushing touchdowns in a game. Asked if he wished he had scored seven, Kamara answered, "Yes."

ARCHIE MANNING—The founding member of the Manning Dynasty, his experience playing for the crappy Saints of the 1970s led him to make sure his sons Peyton and Eli didn't accept being drafted by teams like San Diego and San Diego.

CINCINNATI BENGALS

FOUNDED 1967 (AFL)

Browns cofounder Paul Brown, the man the Cleveland team is named after, became a cofounder of the Bengals after being fired from the Browns (he lost his name in the divorce). After a dark early period when bullies called the team "The Bungles," fortunes improved, and in 2021, the Bengals made it to the Super Bowl. The Bengals' former tormentors have since apologized for their harsh words, as bullies are known to do.

NOTABLE BENGALS

JOE BURROW—With Burrow under center, the Bengals have five playoff wins, the same amount they had in their entire history before drafting him. That first playoff win came in only his second season and ended the longest active playoff win drought in all four major North American sports. Burrow has consequently drawn interest and trade offers from the Detroit Tigers, Sacramento Kings, and Buffalo Sabres.

ANTHONY MUÑOZ—An offensive tackle, he was the first Bengal to be enshrined in the Hall of Fame. The NFL Network ranked him number twelve in their list of the one hundred greatest players. Muñoz was upset about this, believing he should've been ranked number fourteen.

CHAD OCHOCINCO JOHNSON—Originally six-time Pro Bowler Chad Johnson changed his name in 2008 to "Chad Ochocinco" to match his number eighty-five jersey (also on the table was Chad Quatre-Vingt-Cinq, Chad 八十五, and Chad This Many).

TERRELL OWENS—Third in all-time NFL receiving yards and receiving touchdowns, he played for a lot of teams, including the Bengals. As of this writing, Owens is playing for the Knights of Degen in Fan Controlled Football (FCF). In FCF, all the rosters, coaches, and real-time play calling is done by fans using an app. It's thus quite possible that one day, a toddler fiddling with their mommy's phone will accidentally take the Bored Ape FC to the People's Championship.

Aside from his talent, T.O. is famous for his touchdown celebrations, which include:

2000—After scoring against Dallas, he raced to midfield and stood on the Cowboys' logo until Dallas safety George Teague tackled him. In retrospect, Teague should have tried tackling Owens *before* he scored.

2002—He scored a TD, pulled out a marker, signed the ball, and handed it to his financial adviser in the stands. The adviser invested the ball and it's worth more than three balls today.

2006—After a touchdown, he dropped the ball into an oversized Salvation Army Red Kettle. The game was stopped for thirty minutes as the Salvation Army filled out T.O.'s charitable donation tax receipt.

Super Bowls—Some Things That Happened

DAN Before we get into this, let's first acknowledge how lame the name "Super Bowl" is. It's possibly the dumbest title for a major sporting event in history. If "Super Bowl" is the name they went with, what did they reject? "Awesome Bowl"? "The Big Sports-Off"? "Tussle of the Teams"?

In a world of great names like "The World Series" and "The Stanley Cup," the NBA had the common sense to just go with "The NBA Finals." When you think about how simple and child-like "Super Bowl" is, even the NCAA's "Beef O'Brady's Bowl" sounds good by comparison.

Regardless, we know we're stuck with it. Furthermore, the NFL is very litigious about this "great" name, so please pretend in each instance that, instead of "Super Bowl," we've written "Big Game." Also, just to be really safe, maybe read this in the Cayman Islands.

No matter the name, the Super Bowl is an institution—one of the few institutions everyone in America thinks is worthwhile. The 2023 edition was viewed by 113 million people via TV or streaming, and even by some infants who tuned in on their baby monitors. It's a chance for friends and families to gather, fry various foods, and, for some, root for a safety or missed conversion so their crappy "2–8" Super Bowl square has a chance.

Here are some memorable Super Bowl memories:

Super Bowl I

The first ever, in which the Packers beat the Chiefs 35–10. The game was close early on, but then Packer QB Bart Starr took over and his team scored twenty-one unanswered points (even though the points had left voice mails, and followed up with texts).

This was also the only time Roman numerals could be understood since "Super Bowl I" looks like "Super Bowl 1." Never again would anyone who wasn't Roman be able to figure this stupid system out (Roman Gabriel, Bill Romanowski, and Tony Romo are the rare exceptions). We'll use actual numbers going forward both for clarity and to stop Roman numbers from coming into this country and stealing American numbers' jobs.

Super Bowl 20

In Roman numerals, this is XX and, as the number suggests, more "adult" entertainment because this game introduced something children shouldn't be exposed to: the song "The Super Bowl Shuffle." It was recorded by the 1985 Bears as they worked toward the playoffs and was exactly as good as you'd expect cocky football-based rap performed by players to be. It was a surprise hit, however, selling 500,000 copies, and was nominated for a Grammy (category: Super Bowl–based songs). The song proved prophetic as the Bears did win the game, beating the Patriots 46–10.

Super Bowl 26

Buffalo versus Washington. The Bills' amazing offense featured RB Thurman Thomas, and instead of defensive schemes, Washington decided to stop Thomas by hiding his helmet so he couldn't take the field. With help from a private detective, the Bills found the helmet bound and gagged in an airport motel. Thomas only missed two plays, but the Bills were rattled by the experience and lost 37–24.

Super Bowl 2

After trouncing the Raiders 33–14, the Packers carried Coach Lombardi off the field. This should have been an iconic moment, but someone reminded the Packers about the trophy presentation, and they had to sheepishly carry Lombardi back onto the field. After that was over, everyone just walked back to the locker room because, as Packer Willie Davis said, "We couldn't carry him again. He's heavy, and that hat weighs more than you think."

Super Bowl 43

The Cardinals were on the Steelers' one-yard line when QB Kurt Warner's pass was intercepted by James Harrison, who ran it back ninety-nine yards for a touchdown. The Steelers won, and, as of this writing, James Harrison is still trying to catch his breath.

Super Bowl 27

The Cowboys were blowing out the Bills when Dallas tackle Leon Lett recovered a fumble and ran toward the Bills' end zone. At the ten-yard line, he slowed down, holding out the ball to showboat. Bills receiver Don Beebe knocked the ball loose and into the end zone, turning an easy touchdown into a touchback. It could have ruined everything for Dallas, but the Bills were focused on extending their streak of losing Super Bowls, so the Cowboys went on to win the game.

Super Bowl 21

There's disagreement over who first started the Gatorade shower, but it became tradition after the Giants doused Head Coach Bill Parcells in their 1987 Super Bowl win over the Broncos. What there's no disagreement on is the best color Gatorade to dump on a coach. The Supreme Court has ruled (6–3) it's orange.

Super Bowl 47

Baltimore was leading San Francisco 28–6 when the lights in the Superdome went off. Apparently, the Superdome's owner thought his wife was paying the bill, and she thought he was. Anyway, after they had a good laugh, they called the power company and paid with their credit card, the lights came on, and the Ravens held on to win. Still, the real winners that day were the husband and wife, who had a cute story to tell at dinner parties.

Super Bowl 25

One of the most exciting games ever ended with Bills kicker Scott Norwood famously missing a field goal attempt "wide right." But the next day all people were talking about was Whitney Houston's amazing version of the national anthem. Even the headlines read "Giants Beat Bills 20–19 at Whitney Houston Concert."

Super Bowl 52

In a gimmick play against the Patriots, Eagle TE Trey Burton tossed a TD pass to QB Nick Foles. The Eagles went on to win and the play became part of comedian Dane Cook's act: "A quarterback catching a pass? What's next—loose ends? A thin receiver?" (Mr. Cook pauses for laughter that never comes.)

Super Bowl 17

Down 17–13 to the Dolphins with just ten minutes left, Washington was facing fourth-and-one. Joe Theismann handed the ball to John Riggins, who ran forty-three yards, getting not only the first down but also a touchdown, which everyone agreed was better.

Super Bowl 32

John Elway's Broncos were tied with the Packers in the third quarter. Having already lost three Super Bowls, Elway was determined to win this one. On third and six, the thirty-seven-year-old ran and, diving to get extra yards, was hit and spun in the air, parallel to the ground, before landing for the first down. The Broncos went on to win, Elway got his ring, and "Spin the Elway"–in which John Elway comes to a party, is spun violently in the air, and whichever two kids his splayed limbs point at upon landing then have to kiss—remains a popular game for Denver teenagers to this day. It takes a lot of time for the Hall of Famer, but he graciously does it to "give back to the community."

Super Bowl 49

The Catch: The Patriots were leading the Seahawks 28–24 late in the fourth quarter when Seattle QB Russell Wilson stepped back and threw. Patriots defender Malcolm Butler deflected the ball, but it landed on top of Seattle receiver Jermaine Kearse, who was flat on his back on the field. After hitting Kearse's leg, arm, a passing bird, and a series of dominoes that fell in spectacular fashion, the ball settled back into Kearse's hands for one of the greatest catches in Super Bowl history and the only time juggling has proved entertaining.

The Snatch: Kearse's catch kept the Seahawks' drive alive until they were on the Patriots' one-yard line. Wisdom suggested they hand it to their monster running back Marshawn Lynch to pound it in, but this was no time for wisdom. Instead, Wilson tried a pass, and Malcolm Butler—the same Malcolm Butler who had deflected the Kearse pass (really, how many Malcolm Butlers do you think played for the Patriots?)—intercepted it, sealing victory for the Patriots like Tupperware seals in flavor! (This last line sponsored by Tupperware.)

Super Bowl 3

A few days before the game, Joe Namath boldly guaranteed the Jets would win, and they did. Lost in the sands of time are Namath's other predictions that day: *Sonic the Hedgehog* would be a great video game *and* movie, cryptocurrency would be a really great investment until suddenly it wasn't, and at some point, 4, 13, 24, 33, 38, and 43 would be winning lottery numbers.

Super Bowl 42

Giants versus the Patriots—and the Giants needed a play. Eli Manning saw David Tyree streaking across the middle and fired a laser toward him. Just as Tyree caught the ball, he was hit but, miraculously, amazingly, he was able to press the ball against his helmet as he went to the ground. Ruled a catch, it was a key part of the scoring drive that gave the Giants the win. This amazing play instantly became

NFL legend, but what few know is that David Tyree had been preparing for that catch his entire life.

As a young boy in New Jersey, David would lie in bed, envisioning himself making a "helmet catch" to win the Super Bowl. Not content to just dream about it, young David decided to *make* it happen. Every day, in his basement, he'd break open a new "Wooly Willy" toy to collect the iron filings inside. Once he had enough, he'd ride his bike to a ranch outside of town and sprinkle the iron among the grass the grazing cattle ate. Why? Well, David had done his research. Those cows were the ones whose leather would eventually be used by Wilson to make footballs.

On top of feeding cows iron, David was also busy magnetizing his helmet. It caused problems at home when forks stuck to it, along with his retainer and, once, his grandfather's wheelchair, but David persevered, and it paid off. That Super Bowl, when Manning threw the ball toward him, he didn't even need his hands. He was wearing his magnetized helmet, and the football was made from cows full of iron. That catch wasn't even about athleticism. It was about science.

Later than night, after the celebratory champagne, David sat down to a victory meal with his teammates. When his steak tasted a little metallic, he smiled.

Super Bowl 57

It was the first time two African American quarterbacks (Patrick Mahomes and Jalen Hurts) played against each other, and both put up huge numbers, with the Chiefs finally winning 38–35 on a last-second field goal. The game was also known as the "Kelce Bowl" because, for the first time, two brothers played against each other: Travis Kelce on the Chiefs and Jason Kelce on the Eagles. Their mother, Donna, became famous for wearing a combined Eagles-Chiefs jersey, jacket, and hat, and was subsequently sued by both teams for copyright violation. She is currently serving seven years in a federal prison.

The Biggest Super Bowl Halftime Scandals

BROTI GUPTA

The halftime show is the big break in the big game. It's been called the "Super Bowl commercials" of the Super Bowl. But, like every great event, it hasn't gone completely without scandal. Here are some you may not remember, but are nevertheless true. Nobody knows everything—especially you.

Janet Jackson–Gate

Backstage before the famous 2004 Super Bowl halftime show, Justin Timberlake went through his usual pre-performance ritual, asking everyone, "Do you have two nipples?" They all said no, as everyone knew Justin Timberlake was afraid of symmetrical torso parts. Jackson, however, couldn't tell a lie, and when she said yes, Timberlake was rattled. Still shaken, he exposed one of Jackson's breasts during the performance, and seeing it, knowing there was a matching nipple nearby, was too much for Timberlake, who was carried home in a stretcher. All's well that ends well!

M.I.A.–Gate

Oh, M.I.A. Without periods, it's the name "Mia." But with, it's "missing in action." Which was *not* the case with M.I.A. at the 2012 Super Bowl, where she performed and caused quite a controversy. During a dance number, the singer decided she was either going to punch one of the NFL players or give the audience "the devil's thumbs-up." She chose to give everyone the middle finger, which was great news for New York Giants quarterback Eli Manning, who, my sources tell me, "hates to be punched."

Beyoncé-Gate

The rousing performance of "Formation" that Beyoncé gave the world in 2016 was definitely the highlight of that year's halftime show. But wanna know the real reason it was so brief? That's right—Beyoncé double booked herself! The multi-hyphenate superstar had made a dental appointment for the exact time the show was scheduled to begin. Luckily, backstage, a few adult men (and one kindly ghost) formed the band Coldplay and were able to cover for her while she dealt with her orthodontia, saving her from paying the rescheduling fee. She ran over from the dental office with just enough time to perform her hit single retainer-free!

The Green Bay Packers-Gate

As a consolation prize for not being one of the two teams competing in the Super Bowl, the NFL thought it would be nice to invite the Packers to be the halftime musical guest. Well, egg on everyone's face: when the team got onto the field, instead of singing a choral rendition of "Medley from *The Little Mermaid*," they immediately started playing an intersquad game. They even had the audacity to stop midway through to ask, "Who'll be playing halftime for us?" Needless to say, the whole crowd was bored, confused, and angry.

Nepotism-Gate

In 2013, the NFL was under fire for inviting its nephew, Henry, to play trumpet as the halftime show. Henry had recently started playing the trumpet in the school marching band and became medium-good at it. That Henry didn't even play solo trumpet, but rather just the parts all the trumpets were assigned, stung a little bit extra, according to trumpet artists who *don't* have the NFL on their family trees.

Watergate

This one's pretty much as classic a scandal as you can get. Basically, the Nixon administration covered up its involvement in the DNC break-in that happened on June 17, 1972, which led to the resignation of the disgraced president in 1974. But what the media didn't report is that Nixon resigned because he wanted to perform at the next halftime show and was worried being the president would get in the way of rehearsals. The easiest way to get around this? Do exactly one Watergate.

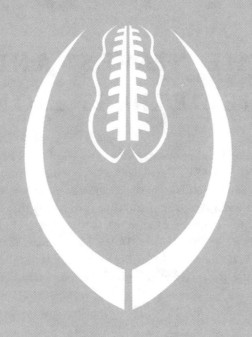

(THE DISPARITY OF) THE

1970s

THE "HAVES" AND
THE DETROIT LIONS

DAN The NFL likes to boast about parity—that any team can beat any other team on "any given Sunday." (William "The Refrigerator" Perry misheard this as "any given sundae.") If the league really believed in parity, however, we wouldn't have Chiefs–Jets games. There are clearly dynasties, and there are teams that are burning garbage barges, and this disparity in parity began in the 1970s. That's when we first saw consistently dominant teams like the Steelers, Dolphins, Raiders, Vikings, Cowboys, and Rams. Of the twenty participants in Super Bowls from 1971 to 1980, those six teams made up seventeen of the slots, and won nine of the ten games. This un-parity is why, after your kids see a horrific blowout and can't sleep, worrying the Ravens defense will come into their bedroom and sack them like a Carolina quarterback, you have the '70s to blame.

1971

In the longest game ever, the Dolphins finally defeat the Chiefs 27–24 in an AFC divisional matchup that takes eighty-two minutes and forty seconds. Bobby Bell celebrates two birthdays over the course of the game, with cake both times. This causes even further delay as, with each cake, Willie Lanier keeps insisting on a "corner piece."

1972—The Miami Dolphins' Perfect Season

They went 14-0 in the regular season and won their playoff games and the Super Bowl, finishing 17-0. This had never happened before, and has never happened since. Every year, the members of that team still pop champagne and celebrate when the last undefeated team loses, proving that, despite their advanced age, these great champions can still be petty.

1972

On December 23, during an AFC divisional playoff game, a play happens that becomes known in NFL lore as the "Immaculate Reception." Like its less consequential prequel, the immaculate conception, this play has become the inspiration for many sermons.

The Immaculate Reception
(Gridiron 3:10)

With Christmas just two days away, Satan was in a foul mood, angrier than even the most constipated hornet. So the Devil called down to Hell's basement apartment where he kept his meanest minions: the Raiders of Oakland. He would use their upcoming playoff game to flaunt his dark magic over all of America's good, honest, recycling-separating flock.

When the game began, the Steelers of Pittsburgh fought valiantly, but as the hour grew late, it seemed darkness would prevail in the House of Three Rivers. Scared, faith waning, people locked their doors and hid behind closed curtains. Then, with just seconds to go, a holy vessel named Terry Bradshaw felt the grace of goodness fill his beefy body. He resolved that Satan's thirst would not be quenched. He took the ball and stepped back, not with fear, but with purpose; saw John Fuqua running his route; and sent the ball aloft on the back of angels' wings. But as Mr. Fuqua reached for it, Satan sent Jack Tatum—a vicious pawn in his downtrodden army—forward. Tatum hit Fuqua, they both hit that football, and it was repelled like Oscar the Grouch trying to get through the pearly gates: "Back to your trash can, Sinner!"

Every loving heart in the nation clenched as that ball seemed doomed to a cold fate, wobbling to a stop alone on the AstroTurf. But manifested out of hope and divinity arose one Franco Harris. Mr. Harris rescued that ball before it hit the ground and gave it a home in his gentle, loving arms. As Satan's Raiders clawed at him, grasped at him, cursed and exhaled their foul 1970s breath at him, he delivered that ball to the promised land.

Cheers went up. Doors were unlocked, curtains were opened, and household tasks that had been ignored too long were suddenly attended to, because good had won over evil. Victory came to the virtuous. The world was good, and not only had Satan been conquered, but also having started the Oakland defense, he had thus been eliminated from his fantasy football playoffs. Hallelujah! Hallelujah! Hallelujah!

1973

O. J. Simpson becomes the first RB to run for 2,000 yards. No player would do it again for eleven years, and only eight players have done it ever. O. J. still, however, holds the record for "best getting away with murder."

1974

"Sudden death" overtime is added to every game. This ideally would have eliminated ties, but now if a game remains tied after fifteen minutes of sudden death, it ends as a tie anyway. So really, it isn't "sudden death," but "possible death with a chance to still live forever hooked up to a machine."

1974

The league's first serious labor dispute occurs when the NFL Players Association organizes a strike during training camp. The strike falls apart forty days later as defectors begin to report to their teams, but the NFLPA covered their embarrassment by insisting this was just a "training camp" for future strikes.

1978

The Super Bowl in the Louisiana Superdome is the first to be played indoors. Fans say it was like other games, except "this one had a roof!"

1978

The NFL extends its season to sixteen games, making another "perfect season" like the 1972 Dolphins had even harder to pull off. Several former Dolphins campaign the league to expand to a seventy-two-game season, "just to be sure."

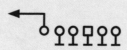

SEATTLE SEAHAWKS

FOUNDED 1974

Having switched conferences in 2002, they're the only team to have played in the AFC *and* NFC Championships. "Seahawks" was chosen in a contest where fans could submit names. Rejected entries included the "Aardvarks" and "Vampires," although the team, trying to soothe any hurt feelings, has reached out to both the aardvark and vampire communities to make sure they feel welcome at all home games.

NOTABLE SEAHAWKS

RUSSELL WILSON—One of only four quarterbacks with a career passer rating over 100, Wilson is also the shortest quarterback to ever win the Super Bowl, a record that seems permanent, unless a quarterback shorter than him comes along.

MARSHAWN LYNCH—Nicknamed "Beast Mode" for his powerful running style, his sixty-seven-yard "Beast Quake" run in the 2010 playoffs against the Saints is considered one of the best ever. Lynch even has a strain of marijuana named after him that claims "It hits you just like Marshawn—hard and fast!" (The effects of the marijuana may vary for different people. Consult your doctor or the kid in the heavy metal jacket at your local high school.)

STEVE LARGENT—A rarity for playing his entire career without the gloves most receivers wear. In retirement, he served in the House of Representatives for eight years—also not wearing gloves, yet this is less of a rarity.

TAMPA BAY BUCCANEERS

The Bucs went 0–14 their first season and had fourteen consecutive losing seasons from 1983 to 1996—all part of a genius plan to bank good karma, which they later cashed in to win two Super Bowls. That karma is depleted now, and the franchise has grand plans to lose a lot in embarrassing ways in the coming years, in order to build up more for their next championship run.

NOTABLE BUCCANEERS

DERRICK BROOKS—An eleven-time Pro Bowler, he's been designated one of the top 100 players in NFL history. That list is now closed, which really sucks for future greats.

WARREN SAPP—A seven-time Pro Bowler, four-time All-Pro, and occasionally controversial figure—especially after a 2002 vicious blindside hit on Packer Chad Clifton away from the play that left Clifton unable to walk for weeks. When Packer coach Mike Sherman yelled at Sapp about the hit, Sapp responded, "Put a jersey on!" Presumably, he meant Sherman should put on an opponent's jersey, but it was a long time ago, so it would be embarrassing to ask for clarification now.

TOM BRADY (AGAIN)—Joined the Bucs in 2020 and won the Super Bowl with them that same season. Things like this are why people say Brady is the greatest to ever play. Our next chapter thinks those people are wrong, and probably ugly.

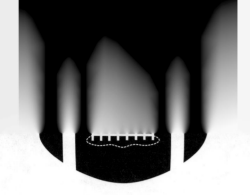

Tom Brady, Worst of All Time (the WOAT)

A Strained Argument in Five Parts

Tom Brady's often called the GOAT, an acronym for "Greatest of All Time." During his career, he piled up Super Bowls, Pro Bowls, and a bunch of other meaningless accomplishments. Why meaningless? Because a true student of the game ignores data. Instead, they contemplate until the truth appears like take-out food—steaming hot and slightly mispackaged. That truth reveals Tom Brady is *not* the Greatest of All Time. He may actually be the worst. Let's let facts explain:

Fact 1: The best players are at their best in close games.

We've all heard the expression "Pressure makes diamonds." Fewer of us have heard the equally valid expression "Pressure makes mashed potatoes." The point is, the best shine when games are close. This suggests that the closest games feature the players that are most best. Well, no games are closer than ones that end in a tie and Tom Brady *never* played in a tie. Len Dawson (eleven ties), Sonny

Jurgenson (eight), Bart Starr (seven), Fran Tarkenton (six), and modern legends like Andy Dalton (two) have, and therefore *they* should be our candidates for the title of GOAT. Brady should instead be known as the OSTRICH: Obviously Suckiest Tie Recorder in Competitive History.

Fact 2: Yes, Brady's won some Super Bowls, but he's also lost a lot.

He played in ten and won seven, meaning he's *lost* three of them, a success rate of a measly 70 percent. QB Trent Dilfer played in one Super Bowl and won one. That's a 100 percent success rate, which is higher. Brady doesn't even hold the record for losing the most Super Bowls, since both Frank Reich and Jim Kelly each lost four. Brady isn't even the greatest at losing. Honestly, what *is* this guy good at?

Fact 3: Brady is no Karlaftis. Not even close.

George Karlaftis, DE, started as a rookie with the Chiefs in 2022 and ended that season winning the Super Bowl. Tom played twenty-three seasons, many ending without a championship. Not George. All George does is win. He doesn't even know how to lose. In fact, he'd have to hire some sort of mentor to teach him to lose. It would be like a master class for failures, and there isn't a better failure instructor than Tom Brady, multiple-time not-winner.

Fact 4: Brady doesn't even think he's the greatest. Why should we?

If Brady thought he was the best, he would have worn uniform number 1. Instead, he wore the bland number 12. People will argue he did that because he's humble, but if so, why not take the most humble number—99? Mark Gastineau wore 99 and all reports suggest he was an incredibly humble player who despised attention.

Fact 5: If he's truly great, would we be jealous?

"True greatness comes only with true sensitivity" (source: Snapple lid). If Brady was "the greatest," he'd understand this points out to others that they *aren't*, and hurting people's feelings isn't something someone great would do. That's why this book is purposefully mediocre—out of respect for the feelings of other books. Tom could learn a lot from this book, but then, couldn't we all?

Conclusion

On football's Mount Rushmore, Tom Brady will only be there if he pays the admission price. Assuming he pays (getting a "senior discount"), Brady can look up at the *true* legends of the game: Dilfer, Dalton, Gastineau, and Karlaftis. (Also George Washington, since, for budget reasons, this Mount Rushmore is just gonna be built on top of the old one.)

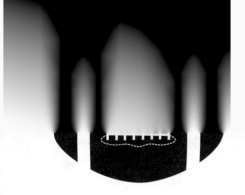

Rivals

DAN The NFL's given fans many great rivalries, such as:

- Giants vs. Cowboys
- Packers vs. Vikings
- Steelers vs. Raiders
- 49ers vs. Rams
- Jerry Jones vs. Jimmy Johnson
- Everyone vs. Al Davis
- Guy sneaking in beer vs. security watching for guys sneaking in beer
- Needing to pee at halftime vs. the long line at the bathroom

The league itself has also had rivals, with the successful ones, the AAFC and the AFL, being absorbed into the NFL. Here are some challengers to the throne who weren't so lucky:

The United States Football League (1983–1986)

The USFL, having lured NFL stars like Jim Kelly, Reggie White, and eventual failed Georgia senatorial candidate Herschel Walker, seemed like a threat to the NFL, but that's like saying matches seemed like a threat to the sun. Even Donald Trump owned a USFL team—the New Jersey Generals—but the team failed (just like Trump Steaks, Trump Airlines, Trump

University, Trump Casinos, and Donald Trump Jr.). The USFL did manage to beat the NFL in one thing: an antitrust lawsuit, winning a total sum of three dollars. One of those dollars went to the lawyers, and the other two were divided among the teams. Even with that financial windfall, the league folded in 1986.

> **NOTE:** A new version of the USFL began play in 2022 but claims to have nothing to do with the old USFL from the '80s. This new league wants to fail and go bankrupt completely on its own merits.

Replacement Players in the NFL (1987)

During the 1987 season, players went on strike and "scabs" played for three weeks before a deal was struck and the union players returned. Washington won the Super Bowl that year, and more than thirty years later, those replacement players were finally actually given championship rings. It had been so long since Washington had won a championship, however, that people there had forgotten how to even put on championship rings. An expert was brought in from the 49ers to teach them.

NFL Europe (1991–1993; 1995–2007)

In 1991, the NFL decided to go to Europe, backpack, stay in hostels, meet friends it would immediately forget, and also start a new league. It lasted two seasons.

In 1995, the league tried again. Hoping to integrate with European culture this time, players wore berets instead of helmets, drank wine instead of Gatorade, and smoked

constantly. Finally, after losing an estimated $30 million per season, the league gave up and slunk back home to its remaining billions.

Starting in 2007, the NFL tried a different approach, letting European cities host regular season games. These games have proven to be a big success with local fans and also some Americans who travel to the games now that "Finally, Europe has something worth seeing."

The XFL (2001)

Founded by WWE's Vince McMahon, the idea behind the XFL was that it would be a "rougher version" of football. Yes, in the era of concussion protocols, the XFL thought the NFL wasn't rough enough. The initial plan to give players machetes and make them turn in three opponents' ears for a field goal (seven for a touchdown, obviously) was eventually revised to just having fewer rules than the NFL. The XFL also allowed players to put nicknames on their jerseys, and soon XFL fans were cheering for "Baby Boy," "Mondo," and "He Hate Me." Even with these advances, the league lasted just one season and lost $70 million. According to rumors, Vince McMahon had a suit jacket made with "Me Hate Money" embroidered on the back.

NOTE: The XFL returned in a new incarnation in 2020 but stopped after five games due to the COVID pandemic. It was then sold to an ownership group that includes Dwayne "The Rock" Johnson and began play again in 2023. If this version fails, there are rumors that the league may be sold to another ownership group that includes the GEICO gecko.

The United Football League (2009–2012)

After watching the failure of the first USFL, this challenger to the NFL's throne identified the problem as too many letters in the league's name. They dropped the "S" and the UFL was born. The league launched with just four teams and quickly collapsed in a flurry of lawsuits.

The Arena Football League (1987–2008; 2010–2019)

Arena football is the rare rival that did find an audience, lasting almost twenty years, and then another ten when reincarnated. Even more impressive, arena football was the launching point for Kurt Warner, Super Bowl-winning quarterback. Warner never won an ArenaBowl Championship, which confirms what many have suggested: the NFL is way easier than arena football.

Arena football players in the 1990s made about $22,000 a year until they unionized and salaries rose to $80,000. Owners, unable to pay pro football players as much as mid-level insurance salesmen, declared bankruptcy in 2009. A couple of years later, they tried again, drastically cutting salaries to $830 per game, with quarterbacks given an extra $250 to fund their flashy quarterback lifestyles. The league couldn't make these astronomical numbers work and folded again.

For fans still craving indoor football, there's now something called the Indoor Football League, or, of course, always the option of watching two kids play in the living room until someone breaks a lamp and their mom gets mad.

The Alliance of American Football (AAF) (2019)

The AAF studied the original XFL and determined its fatal flaw was that the football was bad. They dared ask, "What if the football was *good*?" Even with this bold idea, the league had financial problems and lasted less than one season. Suddenly everyone who had stocked up on Arizona Hotshots merchandise found themselves hosting garage sales with *deep* discounts.

The Canadian Football League (CFL) (1958–present)

The CFL is sort of the Sonic Burgers to the NFL's McDonald's. It counts as a rival only because, between 1993 and 1995, the CFL expanded to the United States, adding teams in Sacramento and San Antonio, and even a team called the Baltimore CFL Colts. The Baltimore team changed their name to the Stallions and, in 1995, won the Grey Cup—the only American team to ever do so.

For the CFL, this was a big deal—the sports equivalent of Miss North Korea being crowned Miss America. And before people say I'm equating Baltimore to North Korea, I'm not. Baltimore has way better lobster rolls.

Right after the Stallions' win, Browns owner Art Modell moved his team to Baltimore, and the champion Stallions were immediately and decisively ignored.

Want to read more about the CFL? Ignoring your answer, see the next page.

You Can't Spell Childhood Trauma Without the Letters C, F, and L

ROBERT COHEN

There is still one thing from my upbringing in Canada that continues to cause me fear and anxiety: Why did the Canadian Football League, consisting of only nine teams, give the same name to two of them? The Saskatchewan Roughriders . . . and the Ottawa Rough Riders.

Seeking solace, I called the CFL office and spoke to the Commissioner, who said he'd have to yell because of the lunch rush. I asked why, and he told me the office was behind a noisy Thai restaurant. So far, on brand.

He explained the Ottawa team was founded in 1876, and their name comes from logging. What could be more Canadian than logging? (Unless the logs were being fired by Wayne Gretzky into nets made out of moose.) The men who helped guide loose logs down rivers were nicknamed "rough riders."

He then explained that in Canada's old west, the Royal Canadian Mounted Police rode horses that were "rough," or unbroken, so they also were known as "rough riders." But since THAT NAME WAS ALREADY TAKEN, Saskatchewan just smushed the words together for their own team name.

My head was spinning. Didn't anyone find it weird when the two teams played each other in the 1966 Grey Cup? The frenzied announcer would scream, "The Rough Riders intercept the Roughriders pass, run it back . . . touchdown Rough Riders! It's now Rough Riders 10, Roughriders 27!" Bananas.

I told the Commissioner the CFL blew any legitimacy the second they made this silly decision, but then I realized the other end of the phone had been silent for quite a while. The line was dead. In that silence, it suddenly hit me. Two teams sharing the same name may be the most Canadian thing ever. It's weird, but connected to our weird history as a nation. Instead of fighting it, I should embrace it. I love Canada, and this was as "Canada" as things get.

EPILOGUE: Eventually the Commissioner called me back from a payphone and explained our call ended because the CFL's budget only gave execs disposable cell phones with ten pre-paid minutes. I thanked him, and we may talk again next fiscal year when the minutes refresh. If we do, it will be quick.

THE

1980s

A DECADE BETWEEN
THE '70S AND '90S

DAN If you look online for "The 1980s," you'll learn that this is when entertainment took off—video games, music videos, cable TV, and so on. The '80s were also when the NFL's entertainment level took off, with high-powered offenses led by star quarterbacks. Of this decade's ten NFL MVPs, seven were quarterbacks. Also, before 1980, there were only two seasons in which a QB threw for 4,000 yards (Joe Namath in '67 and Dan Fouts in '79), but in the 1980s, there were fourteen, fueled by players with last names like Elway, Montana, and Marino. We'd love to publish their first names, but ink is expensive.

Thanks to all this offense, football cemented its place over baseball as America's favorite sport. Baseball, if you're not familiar with it, is that sport where people stand around and nothing happens. It's like a high school dance, but at high school dances, occasionally someone scores.

1982

"The Catch"– Down by six, time dwindling, and eighty-nine yards away from the end zone in the NFC Championship Game, Joe Montana went to work. He moved the 49ers to the Dallas six-yard line. From there, he took the snap and rolled right, with three defenders approaching fast. Seemingly trapped, seemingly desperate, Montana threw over Ed "Too Tall" Jones (who clearly wasn't tall enough) and found a leaping Dwight Clark for a touchdown that sent the 49ers onward to their first Super Bowl win in one of the most iconic plays in NFL history. It ended the Cowboy dynasty, started the 49ers dynasty, and had no real effect on the TV show *Dynasty*, which had already been on for a year.

1984

Eric Dickerson sets the record for most rushing yards in a season (2,105).

1987

Players go on strike for twenty-four weeks and owners use replacement players, who deliver an inferior product to fans. In 1995, during an owners' strike, the league used replacement owners, and no one noticed or cared.

1987

"The Drive"—The Broncos were losing to Cleveland by seven with five minutes left in the AFC Championship Game. Broncos QB John Elway took his team ninety-eight yards in fifteen plays to tie the game, and the Broncos eventually won in overtime to go to the Super Bowl.

The 1995 Owners' Strike

DAN If you like fairy tale endings, don't look up how the Broncos did in that Super Bowl. Or find a different fairy tale, where the hero almost wins but gets beaten by the New York Giants.

1988

"The Fog Bowl"—During an Eagles/Bears playoff game, a dense fog rolled into Soldier Field. Visibility dropped, and even though Eagles QB Randall Cunningham had 407 passing yards, they couldn't score a TD and lost 20-12. The game was named number three on the list of the NFL's top ten weather games, which is for some reason an actual list.

In truth, this was actually a game in the National Fog League. The Chicago Haze were hosting the St. Louis Peasoupers when a bunch of people showed up and ruined everything. In the world of fog, they call this game "The People Bowl."

Photo of one of the most incredible moments of the Fog Bowl.

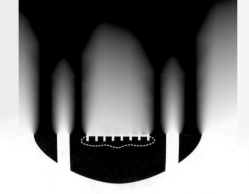

Maybe YOU Could Play in the NFL!

(You Probably Can't)

After reading this far into this book, it's natural to wonder, *Could I play in the NFL?*

Well, playing pro football can't be learned just by reading a book, the way heart surgery or pro baseball can. Also, being old enough to read suggests it's already too late. You needed to get started earlier, ideally before you were born.

Genetics are a huge factor in how likely someone is to play pro football. The laziest of research suggests there've been 130 NFLers whose fathers also played. There are also five players who are third-generation pros. The best DNA clearly belongs to the Matthews family—they've produced seven pros over three generations, more than every New York Jets draft combined.

NOTE: With time to reflect, we've come to realize the above Jets joke is mean-spirited, yet accurate. We therefore both apologize for it and stand by it.

So, if you're serious about making the league, your best chance is to try to be born into the Matthews family. If this doesn't work, and it can't because it's impossible, don't worry—you can still salvage your pro career. You just need to burst out of the womb with the energy of Ray Lewis coming out of the tunnel, because football training for kids starts as young as eighteen months.

We've seen many two-year-olds who didn't get into the system early enough be tagged as busts, then have to scramble around for backup careers like lawyer or tech billionaire.

Hopefully you started working out in daycare, because you'll need to be in game shape by the time you turn three. That's when most organized leagues start—first with flag football, and then, at age five or six, with tackle. Even that young, coaches are looking for maturity. They want to know their players are crying because they broke their tiny little collarbones, not having a tantrum because the other team isn't "sharing" the football.

The most prominent kids football organization is the Pop Warner League (named after the old man himself), which started in 1929. Estimates are between 60 and 70 percent of all NFL players played Pop Warner. Part of the appeal is that Pop Warner has no tryouts and anyone that signs up gets to play, just like with the New York Jets.

NOTE: This is getting really cruel. We should stop.

NOTE: We probably won't.

For safety, Pop Warner kids only play against other kids the same weight. This rule was instituted after a six-year-old fullback in Texas who weighed 300 pounds started plowing through defenders and "putting up some serious numbers."

DAN The kid could have made it all the way if a scout at one of his middle school games hadn't given him free orange slices and ruined his eligibility.

The next step is high school football. Be warned, though, high school teams want something both college and NFL teams also look for: actual ability. So, if you can, make sure you have that. Playing in high school means you'll get better coaching, access to weight rooms, and, according to every movie from the 1980s, to date the head cheerleader. And if you're good enough in high school, you can move on to college ball.

The NFL, like hedge funds, won't even look at you unless you went to college. Where hedge funds want graduates from Harvard, Yale, and Princeton, NFL teams prefer players from schools like Penn State, Alabama, and even something called Florida Atlantic University (basically a hairdressing school in a strip mall).

According to *Forbes* (and who knows football better?), in 2019 about one million kids played high school ball (probably not all on the same team), but only about 30,000 play Division I college football. That's a much smaller number. Still, if you've shown your skills in high school are good enough to play in college, and you've shown your skills in college are good enough to play pro, you will get an invite to . . . show your skills again, this time at the combine.

The annual National Invitational Camp, known as the NFL Scouting Combine, started in 1982 in Tampa, but since 1985 it has been held in Indianapolis. If you are in Indianapolis, and have already visited the Children's Museum and Fountain Square, you can't just show up to the combine. NFL teams choose who comes, and in 2022, they only invited 324 players. Since only 262 get drafted, this makes the combine the NFL version of *Squid Game*. (This *Squid Game* reference will most likely be out of date by the time you read it, because it was already out of date the moment it was written.)

At the combine, players are evaluated on things like:

Forty-yard dash—Also known as "running." The fastest time ever posted was in 2017, when John Ross ran 4.22 seconds. He was drafted by Cincinnati and used that blazing speed to embarrass slower teammates coming onto the field pre-game. After some stern conversations with the offensive line, Ross now gives them all head starts.

Bench-pressing 225 pounds as many times as possible—Justin Ernest, a defensive tackle, set the record in 1999 with fifty-one times. He was never drafted because no one likes a show-off.

Vertical jump—Safety Gerald Sensabaugh set the record of forty-six inches in 2005. In his rookie year with the Jacksonville Jaguars, he had twenty-four defensive tackles *and* was voted "Most Valuable Player for Getting Stuff Off of High Shelves."

Broad jump—In 2015, cornerback Byron Jones set not only the combine record, but also the *world* record by jumping 12'3". Sadly, he jumped before the whistle and was called offsides.

The Wonderlic test—Named after its creator, Eldon Wonderlic, this series of multiple-choice questions evaluates cognitive ability and problem solving. Only one player ever got a perfect score: punter Pat McInally, in 1975. This comes as no surprise when you realize McInally was a graduate of Harvard, where he studied useless test taking. Eventually, even the NFL realized the test was useless and have stopped giving it as of 2022.

Height, weight, arm length, and hand span—Teams learn the dimensions of players, collecting all the measurements needed to surprise them with a custom-made tuxedo.

Interviews—Teams ask prospects about the game and their families, and, like most TV talk show interviews, prospects get a chance to promote upcoming movies or albums.

Drug screening—This isn't to see *if* players are using drugs, but rather to see, if they are using them, *how well* they're using them. Champions do everything to the best of their ability.

Even if you kill it at the combine, you may not get drafted. If that happens, you can relax knowing that teams still invite many undrafted free agents to training camp and lots end up playing pro. In fact, 30 percent of players in the NFL were undrafted, including seventeen Hall of Famers. You want names? How about these:

Adam Vinatieri—Imagine it's the finals, everything's on the line, and then you come up against the one thing certain to end your amazing run: Adam Vinatieri. In this scenario, you aren't playing against his team in the Super Bowl; you're onstage at your school's spelling bee and you need to spell his name to win. Can a name have that many "i's" in it? Is that legal? Vinatieri was just as scary on the field. A four-time Super Bowl champ, he holds almost every kicking record there is, and was recognized as one of the best 100 NFL players ever.

Wes Welker—Not just a great receiver for twelve years, he also gave the greatest interview in NFL history after Jets coach Rex Ryan's wife posted a foot fetish video. Welker went out of his way to make as many foot references as possible, including "putting our best foot forward," "need to be on your toes," and "It's a playoff atmosphere. You can't just stick your toe in the water." He made eleven in total—which is one reference for every toe, if we're talking about a foot with an extra toe (also known as a foot giving it "110 percent").

Nate Newton—A three-time Super Bowl champ who is recognized as one of the best guards in history, he also made headlines in retirement by getting arrested with 213 pounds of marijuana in his van. Just weeks later, he was arrested again with 175 pounds of marijuana. Give the guy credit—he was trying to clean up his act, just not fast enough. (Who expects guards to be fast?)

Also never drafted–Drew Pearson, Priest Holmes, Joe Jacoby, Antonio Gates, Tony Romo, Warren Moon, and Kurt Warner.

Reading names this impressive, you're probably hoping you *don't* get drafted, but if you unfortunately do, console yourself with the fact that NFL rookies earn salaries of around $705,000. That's the income of a good doctor or a bad embezzler.

If you do make it to the NFL, congrats–you beat the odds. Remember those one million high school players in 2019? Each of them had around a tiny fraction of a percent chance to make it. A tiny fraction of a percent is also the likelihood of being hit by lightning or how much cheapskates tip waiters. (Be aware that if you do only tip a tiny fraction of a percent, there is a high likelihood you will be hit by your waiter.)

Now that you're in the bigs, have fun. Play as yourself in *Madden*, buy your grandmother a gold-plated jet ski, but also know the ride can be over quick. Players get cut more often than beef at Benihana. They get waived more than a "surrender" flag in France. (We know that's not how you spell "waved" but maybe it's how you spell it in France?) The average NFL career is only about two and a half years, and since most players start at twenty, this means most are done by twenty-three.

If this was you, and you're now twenty-three and out of the only job you ever wanted, what do you do now? LinkedIn (like Facebook, but with only half as many conspiracy theories) studied players' post-football careers and found that:

- 20 percent own small businesses or are entrepreneurs
- 18 percent are in sales
- 9 percent are in coaching or are fitness professionals
- 8 percent are in finance/insurance/banking

- 5 percent work with athletics departments, either on school campuses or professionally
- 3 percent are in media and sports broadcasting
- 3 percent are in education
- 34 percent are "other"

DAN Looking at these numbers, it's obvious that a lot of people who play in the NFL don't even care about football. They just do it because they know it's the best way to have their dream career as an "other." But that's not you. We could tell the moment we pretended to meet you. You love the game and now, in our hypothetical scenario, you're not ready to give it up. Well, it's exactly for warriors like you that we'd like to propose one other option for former players: **The NFL Senior League.**

Golf has one, so why not football? After all, both sports use balls and have guys named "Phil." A senior league would be a chance for fans to watch their old favorites pick up the pads (and knee braces and sometimes walkers) one more time. Wouldn't it be great seeing our heroes make "old man noises" as they bend over to snap the ball? Put on bifocals to read the tiny writing on those QB armbands with plays on them? Try to leave the game early to "beat the traffic"? This idea is offered here free to any investors eager to lose their money.

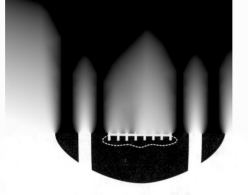

The Point of Points

With Raber Analytics

Points are important. They tell us the score and let us know how badly we lost our bets.

But points don't just exist in football—they're in *every* sport. That epiphany led us to wonder: How do football points compare in value to points in other sports? Which then led to another question: What if each sport's points were like currencies, and we set up one of those little foreign exchange booths you see in the airport to convert them while also screwing travelers on rates and commissions?

Figuring all this out seemed like a tough task, but as bad cooks say about their Jell-O, "It's only tough because it's protecting the juicy meat inside." Driven to figure all of this out but also lazy, we hired sports data firm Raber Analytics to compare and convert different sports' points. Their name rhymed with the famous Saber Analytics, so we knew they must be great. The same logic will let you save money on a trip to "Spain" by instead visiting the much more affordable Fort Wayne.

It was a thankless assignment for Raber Analytics. They had to make several assumptions and ignore important realities to produce results meant only for entertainment or endless discussion on midafternoon sports talk shows. Here's what they found:

League	Average Points Per Game	Average Points Per Team Per Game	Relative Value of Single Point	Single Point Value Relative to Single NFL Point
NFL	47.2	23.6	0.042	-
English Premier League (EPL) (Soccer)	2.68	1.34	0.746	**17.612**
NBA	222.8	111.4	0.009	**0.212**
MLB	9.2	4.6	0.217	**5.130**
NHL	5.98	2.99	0.334	**7.893**
National Rugby League	45.8	22.9	0.044	**1.031**

This means an NHL goal is roughly eight times more valuable than a point in the NFL, while a basket in the NBA is worth much less.

To convert all this into currencies, let's set $1 USD equal to one touchdown (assumed to be 7 points):

Points as Currency Touchdown = $1.00 USD	
NFL Touchdown (7 points)	$ 1.00
NBA Free Throw (1 point)	$ 0.03
NBA Two-Pointer	$ 0.06
NBA Three-Pointer	$ 0.09
NBA Twenty-Point Game	$ 0.61
MLB R (Single)	$ 0.73
MLB Grand Slam	$ 2.92
EPL Goal	$ 2.52
NHL Goal	$ 1.13
NHL Hat Trick	$ 3.39

Now that we have a common language—money—we see that:

- Tyler Lockett's eight TDs in 2021 (an $8 value) were worth roughly the same as the NBA's Jock Landale's 265 points. Tyler Lockett may want to mention this to the Seahawks since he only made $2 million while Landale made over $2.2 million. Don't those owners understand value?

- Alvin Kamara's six TDs in 2020 against the Vikings were more valuable than *any single-game performance in NBA history*—even Wilt Chamberlin's 100-point game ($3.05 compared to Kamara's $6). It was as if Kamara scored 200 NBA points, which would have probably made some news.

- LeBron's career average of 27.1 points per game is roughly equivalent to Derrick Henry averaging 0.81 TDs per game, or Cristiano Ronaldo's EPL average of 0.44 goals per game. Despite this equivalency, the NBA has recognized LeBron as MVP four times while continuing to ignore both Ronaldo and Henry.

- LaDainian Tomlinson's 2006 thirty-one TD season ($31) was more valuable than *any* player's season in NBA history, but it was only a third as valuable as Wayne Gretzky's ninety-two goal season in 1981/82 (worth $104!). Reading this, everyone who cheered for Tomlinson that year probably feels pretty dumb.

So What Does All of This Really Mean?

Well, three things:

1. When people said that every possible statistic in sports had already been dissected, they were wrong.
2. All those players who never score (linebackers, hockey goalies, pitchers, almost every soccer player) are incredibly overpaid. Based on the logic here, they add no value and could be fired and the teams will do just fine. Is this how sabermetrics works?
3. Wayne Gretzky is the greatest NFL player ever.

THE
1990s

THE NFL ON CRUISE CONTROL

DAN While Americans were collecting Beanie Babies, Jerry Rice, Terrell Davis, and Barry Sanders were collecting yards in receiving and rushing. The yards proved much more valuable, as Beanie Babies quickly turned into things people threw away or gave out instead of Halloween candy (and tasted horrible). The league also expanded to Jacksonville, the Carolinas, and Houston, and the Browns became the Baltimore Ravens. The '90s were also when the Cowboys were bought by Jerry Jones, giving him what every billionaire wants: a place to make all their bad decisions.

1993

The second biggest comeback in NFL history occurs in a playoff game between the Bills and Oilers. Down by thirty-two in the third quarter, the Bills score five unanswered touchdowns and a field goal to win. Details have been lost to time, but the few facts historians have cobbled together suggest Bills players and fans were "pleased" with this turn of events.

1994

Philadelphia QB Randall Cunningham punts eighty yards on a quick-kick against Dallas. The punt was the second longest in Eagles history but the first longest in Eagles QB punting history.

1997

The NFL plays its 10,000th game! And presumably has a lifetime record of 10,000 wins and 10,000 losses (ties ignored for the purposes of this exceptional joke).

1997

Vikings QB Brad Johnson throws a pass, which is deflected—and Johnson catches *his own pass* and runs it in for a TD. Finally, the NFL uses the play every little kid tries in his backyard. Maybe the one where you hide the ball under your shirt is next?

CAROLINA PANTHERS

FOUNDED 1993

They went to the NFC Championship Game in only their second year, then didn't have another winning season until 2003, when they lost the Super Bowl to the Patriots. The Panthers did manage to tie the Patriots in the least important statistic ever: teams that claim to represent multiple states. To date, their appeal for a trophy for this (ideally a giant, golden map) has not yielded any results.

NOTABLE PANTHERS

CAM NEWTON—The record holder for quarterback rushing TDs, he was also the first rookie to throw for 4,000 yards in a season and the first to throw for 400 yards in his NFL debut. His famous "Superman" celebration is loved by fans, but proved to be a constant problem when Lex Luthor coached the Panthers (2012 to 2015).

STEVE SMITH SR.—A five-time Pro Bowler and master at trash talk. When he played for the Ravens, he said, "When I think of a Baltimore Raven, what I think of is, we go in there, we take your lunchbox, we take your sandwich, we take your juice box, we take your applesauce, and we take your spork and break it. And we leave you with an empty lunch." This troubled many moms, who worried about the lack of vegetables in the hypothetical lunch.

SIR PURR—The only mascot to ever play in an actual game when, in 1996, he jumped on a live punt, turning it into a touchback. Some other (real) stats from the Panthers website:

- **Weight:** Weight . . . That's Purr-sonal!
- **Major:** Purr-Forming Arts
- Averages over 7 million smiles annually

Transcript of Sir Purr's Hall of Fame Induction Speech

As the only mascot to actually play the game, it makes sense that Sir Purr was inducted into the Hall of Fame. Here is a transcript of the speech Sir Purr gave at his Hall of Fame induction ceremony:

I recognize I'm the first mascot to receive this honor, and I'm overwhelmed. I also must acknowledge the things I've done in my career that I'm less proud of. Mistaking the end zone for a litter box is one. Mistaking it ten more times is ten more. Ultimately, however, I know I've brought mild entertainment to fans for decades, and isn't that more than can be said about the Cleveland Browns players enshrined here? I am—

(*Speech cut off as Sir Purr was viciously tackled by Ozzie Newsome*)

JACKSONVILLE JAGUARS

FOUNDED 1993

The Jags made the playoffs four of their first five seasons, yet still remain one of four teams to never play in the Super Bowl. (If you're curious who the other three are, so are we. If you find out, please tell us.) Controversy arose when the team's mascot, an actual jaguar, got loose while they were playing the Seahawks, who also had a live mascot, and the law of the jungle ran its course.

DAN If you're reading this, please remove your hat in a moment of silence for a good mascot taken too soon.

RIP SQUAWKY, 1998–2001
MAY YOUR MEMORY LIVE ON IN OUR HEARTS
AND IN JIMMY JAGUAR'S STOMACH.

NOTABLE JAGUARS

FRED TAYLOR–His total career yardage is fifteenth in league history–which may not sound like much, but it's more than O. J. Simpson's and John Riggins's. Don't you feel bad laughing about it now? Don't apologize to us, apologize to Mr. Taylor. And look him in the eye when you do it.

JIMMY SMITH–Had seven straight seasons with 1,000 yards receiving and by far the best receiver in team history. You think we'd mention the sixth best receiver? No way–this book is all about the most easily accessible data. We believe the literary term is "low-hanging fruit."

TONY BOSELLI—The first player ever drafted by the Jags and considered their best pick ever. Especially right after they had made that pick.

BALTIMORE RAVENS

FOUNDED 1996

Many think the team name is in honor of Edgar Allan Poe (buried in Baltimore), but it's actually a tribute to the Disney Channel show *That's So Raven*, which many fans found more entertaining than early Ravens games. Who wants to see a one-yard run when they can watch the episode "Campaign in the Neck," where Raven lobbies for her friend Chelsea to become student president?

NOTABLE RAVENS

RAY LEWIS—Considered the greatest middle linebacker in history, he holds the records for most combined tackles and solo tackles. A true force of nature, his movements were tracked by the National Weather Service.

JONATHAN OGDEN—A Super Bowl champion, eleven-time Pro Bowler, and nine-time All-Pro. He was the first Hall of Fame inductee who spent his entire playing career with the Ravens—also leading to his induction into the Homebody Hall of Fame (instead of a yellow jacket, new members are given slippers and a Netflix subscription).

ED REED—Holds the record for career interception return yards (1,590). Reed was known for his ability to lure quarterbacks into throwing interceptions using shiny fishing lures and saying things like, "Bet you can't throw it here. I dare you to."

HOUSTON TEXANS

FOUNDED 1999

Previously the Maui Texans, the Omaha Texans, and the Guam Texans, once they moved to Houston, fans said the name just "feels more right." They're the only franchise to have never won a road playoff game, probably because they don't sleep well in hotel beds. Team management thinks it has something to do with the pillows.

NOTABLE TEXANS

J. J. WATT—A probable Hall of Famer, a force on the field, and a hero off of it, he raised more than $37 million for hurricane relief after Houston was hit by Hurricane Harvey. Watt is thus the closest thing the NFL has to the Dalai Lama (and not just because the Dalai Lama was also rarely on a team that made the playoffs).

DEANDRE HOPKINS—Set a record by hauling in 789 catches before the age of thirty. This record is surprising because quarterbacks usually feel safer throwing to older, established receivers in their fifties or sixties who have had decades in the game and "know what to do."

ARIAN FOSTER—Holds Texans records for rushing yards and rushing touchdowns. He led the league in 2010 with 1,616 yards and 16 touchdowns, which makes perfect sense since it's 100 yards to get a touchdown and $16 \times 100 = 1{,}600$. This logic is rock solid and cannot be disputed.

ANDRE JOHNSON—Holds Texans records in receiving yards, touchdowns, and receptions. He's a member of the Texans Ring of Honor alongside other elite players and an armadillo that sort of looked like a football when it rolled itself up.

Operation: Football Fan

MICHAEL PRICE

If there's one thing my late father loved as much as he loved my mom, us kids, and yelling at the TV whenever Red Skelton came on, it was football. He played in high school and, after his Navy service in World War II, was a defensive back on the semi-pro Cranford (New Jersey) Clippers. By the time I came around, Dad was a fan of the New York Jets—though it's more accurate to say he suffered with the Jets. He berated them, shook his head in disgust, and called them "a bunch of donkeys." Still, Willie Price was determined to pass on his love of football to his four sons. Surely one of us would play like he had when he was young. At the very least, we'd join him in rooting on the Jets.

The plan got off to a rocky start with my big brother. Tim was a bit of a rebel and liked the Beatles more than football—or sports of any kind. This aggravated my dad to no end. I have a specific childhood memory of Dad watching the Beatles perform "Hello, Goodbye" on *The Ed Sullivan Show*, and seeing him bark at the TV, "Hello, goodbye, goodbye, hello, stop, go? What the hell kind of song is that?" Tim was a no-go. That meant I was next up.

I wasn't crazy about sports either. I loved television, watching just about any old cartoon or episode of *The Monkees* I could get my eyes on. But Willie was gonna try anyway. So, one cold December Sunday, my dad did something he hated with every fiber of his being: he drove to New York City. To TV-obsessed me, New York was glamour and excitement—Bugs Bunny lived there! To my dad, New York was dirty and dangerous. Still, he piled me in the car and drove me deep into Queens so I could see the great Joe Namath lead his beloved Jets against the Dolphins at old Shea Stadium.

Here is what happened that day (I looked it up): the Jets won 35–17. Here is what I remember from that day: the men's bathroom. I was about a month short of my ninth birthday, and I had never been to a place like this. I had never seen any other man than my dad up close and personal. And the men's room at old Shea Stadium was the very definition of "up close and personal." The urinal was one big, long metal trough, like what pigs eat out of. So little me waded into a crowd of old men (to a kid, anyone over fifteen is an old man) with cigars in their mouths, their zippers open, and these giant horrific *things* coming out of their pants.

So, no, my experience seeing the Jets play did not turn me into a fan. Nor was I transformed into a player by Dad signing me up the following summer for a "Kids Football Camp" run by our town's parks department. The camp was led by a bullet-headed guy with a marine crew cut who made us stand in the hot sun and hold our arms to our chests in the old-time "blocking stance." I never once touched a ball. Or another kid. When Dad came home from his construction company job that night, I begged him to let me quit. He sighed and said it was okay, and as he went upstairs to change out of his work clothes, I happily plopped down in front of a rerun of *The Munsters*.

The story might have ended there, but then—miraculously—I became a football fan. A rabid "watch every game I can" fan.

Just not of the Jets.

One day at lunch at John F. Kennedy Elementary, I saw the kid next to me doodling on the picture of George Washington on the standard-issue brown paper book cover of *Adventures in Mathematics*. The printed image of the Father of Our Country looked odd: He was smoking a big cigar, and his powdered wig was obscured by a football helmet. A helmet with an amazing design: a big curving horn, like what a giant sheep would have.

"That's 'cuz it's the LA Rams," the kid said.

My mind reeled. The helmet made it look like the guy wearing it had *actual horns*! This was a breakthrough. It made the Jets helmet look like the work of a baby. All it had was a green football with the word "Jets" inside it. Footballs aren't green! But this Rams helmet—this was something else. Just like that, I was a Rams fan. First, the helmet—so cool. Second, they played in Los Angeles. That's where the Monkees lived! Third, their players—Roman Gabriel, Merlin Olsen, Jack Young-blood. These were names out of a comic book. Who did the Jets have, aside from Broadway Joe? Don Maynard. George Sauer. Weeb Ewbank. Come on!

My fate was sealed. And, as it turned out, so were the fates of my two kid brothers, and the fate of my dad's quest to create a Jets fan in his image.

My brother Pat and I get along great these days, but back then he loved to needle me and get under my skin. So, once he learned I was a Rams fan, he—who had no previous interest in football—decided to become a fan of whatever team the Rams played next. And that December 1969, the Rams (my Rams!) went to the Western Conference Championship game against the Minnesota Vikings. To Patrick's glee and my despair, Joe Kapp led the Vikings to a heart-stopping 23–20 win. Pat proceeded to dance around the house celebrating the victory of his new favorite team ever.

Our youngest brother, Billy, was only four years old, but he and I were close, so he decided he'd be a Rams fan to help soothe the hurt of my crushing loss. Mean-while, my dad, who had just seen his beloved donkeys fail to defend their Super Bowl championship, sat there watching us, wondering what the hell just happened to him. In one afternoon, he had lost his three remaining sons to other teams.

To this day, Pat is still a die-hard Vikings fan, and Billy is a Rams fan who has followed them from LA to Anaheim to Saint Louis, and back to LA again. I, on the other hand, had drifted away from football fandom altogether by the time I got out of high school. I never spoke to Dad about my betrayal, and I hope it didn't cause him too much pain. He's been gone for fifteen years now, and though I don't follow football closely anymore, I still spend a little bit of every fall rooting for Gang Green. That "little bit" usually ends around Week Three, by which time the Jets' season is essentially over.

That's when I pay the ultimate honor to Willie Price's memory, by looking at the NFL scores on ESPN and muttering under my breath a single word: "Donkeys!"

THE

200⊙s

AND BEYOND

HEAVY IS THE HEAD THAT WEARS THE HELMET

DAN If history has taught us anything, it's that no one wants to take a history course. They're boring. People would much rather study coding, or sports blooper-ology. Still, history has survived over time, and it reminds us that empires are fragile. The NFL rules the sports universe now, but, as happened to the Roman Empire, the British Empire, and the *Fast & Furious* movie franchise, problems are starting to arise:

Player safety—The physical toll of the game, including concussions and their disastrous long-term effects, have been well profiled, with part of the blame lying with a league that pressures players to play hurt. Unlike the complicated issues in society, player safety isn't easily solved, but hopefully changes in rules and equipment can give fans the action we love without the injuries we hate.

Since 2011, NFL players who get hit in the head have had to go through a process known as the "concussion protocol." Before this, however, anyone who had their bell rung was simply diagnosed on the field by a trainer asking them questions like:

1920s—When does Daylight Savings Time begin, and what the hell's the point of it?

1930s—What is the Tennessee Valley Authority?

1950s—Name the Yankees' starting rotation, in order of who's most over-paid.

1970s—List four John Wayne movies and another eight he's considering.

1990s—What's "grunge" music and how do I stop my son from liking it?

2000s—What should I buy my partner for their birthday? It should look expensive, but not be.

Labor unrest—Franchise value is sky-high, TV brings in billions, and every facet of the league wants their share. Without delicate negotiations (on this and a multitude of other labor issues), the commissioner could face a player lockout, a referee lockout, and, if he forgets his keys in his house, a personal lockout.

Reputation—Fans often see players and ex-players associated with criminal activity, including domestic violence. The fact is, the proportion of NFL players with criminal records is lower than the average population, and has been decreasing since 2006. Still, the attention that high-profile offenders get, combined with the league's weak policies when it comes to punishing those offenders, adds to the stigma.

It's not just players either. The owners, too, have had their share of legal troubles: think Daniel Snyder, Robert Kraft, and many, many others. (Keep hitting the "refresh" button on this book to update this list.)

Racism—A recurring problem, the issue of racism flared up again in 2022 when Brian Flores, one of very few Black head coaches in the league, sued the NFL for discrimination, backed up by a text mistakenly sent to him by Patriots Coach

Belichick. Belichick texts like the Patriots lose and how the league hires qualified Black coaches—poorly. The proof is on the field: of thirty-two teams, only four have a Black head coach. From 2012 to 2021, fifty-one of sixty-two head coaching hires (82.25 percent) were white, even though 71 percent of players are people of color. Those numbers are even worse than Belichick's texting skills. Coach Belichick, if you disagree, text us; we're sure it'll go to your dry cleaner anyhow.

★★★ HISTORICAL HISTORY ★★★

The Music City Miracle

In a 2000 AFC wildcard game, with just seconds left, the Titans had only one chance to come back against Buffalo—a kick return. On the return, the Titans' Frank Wycheck threw a lateral across the field to Kevin Dyson, who ran seventy-five yards to score. The play was dubbed "The Music City Miracle," and is much more revered than "The Music City Debacle," which refers to that time an eight-year-old in the store Music City threw up into a tuba.

2001

"The Tuck Rule"—In the AFC divisional game, Tom Brady seems to fumble after being hit by the Raiders' Charles Woodson, but the officials—shockingly, confusingly—decide Brady hadn't fumbled but was instead moving his arm forward, making it a throw, even though he was "tucking it" into his body. The "fumble" is instead called an incomplete pass, the Patriots go on to win, and no one understands why.

The Tuck Rule—A Very Short Play

CURTAIN OPENS revealing TWO FOOTBALL FANS in front of a TV.

FOOTBALL FAN 1:
Wait, did he actually fumble?

FOOTBALL FAN 2:
No, I guess he didn't.

FOOTBALL FAN 1:
But why did everyone's eyes see that he clearly did?

2004

Peyton Manning throws his forty-ninth touchdown, breaking Dan Marino's 1984 record of forty-eight. Angry, Marino blocks Manning on social media.

> **2007**—Tom Brady throws his fiftieth touchdown, breaking Peyton Manning's record. Manning blocks Brady on social media, but a spiteful Marino starts following Brady and liking all his posts.
>
> **2013**—Peyton Manning throws his fifty-fifth touchdown, breaking Tom Brady's record. Brady blocks Manning on social media. Marino is unsure what he's supposed to do now.

2007

The Michael Vick dogfighting scandal. Vick went bankrupt, then to jail, before coming back to play again for several teams including, sadly, the Jets. Hadn't the man already paid enough for his crimes?

2010

Brett Favre ends his consecutive game streak of 297 games played. Sitting on the bench and learning he still gets paid even if he doesn't play, Favre sarcastically comments to teammates, "Thanks for telling me earlier, guys."

2016

Colin Kaepernick doesn't stand for the national anthem in protest of racial injustice and police brutality. Many players, fans, and media praise him for his bravery. Others boo him or much, much worse. When Kaepernick became a free agent in 2017, no team signed him, even though he had led the 49ers to the Super Bowl. He filed a grievance against the league owners, suggesting collusion to not sign him. As all innocent parties do, in 2019 the NFL settled, and also, like all innocent parties do, insisted the settlement remain confidential.

2021

The league expands the regular season to seventeen games. This made it easier to break records like rushing yards/season and passing yards/season, and also, of course, the record for number of games per season (set in 2021 at seventeen).

Vikings vs. Bills—A New Game for the Ages

Of all the "Greatest Games Ever Played," the Bills–Vikings matchup on November 13, 2022, was the most recent. The Bills were up by 4 with less than a minute left, but the Vikings were one yard away from a touchdown. When the Bills stopped them cold, statistics declared they had a win expectancy of 99.9 percent. What that percentage didn't account for, however, was events happening. Trying to run out of their end zone, the Bills fumbled, and the Vikings recovered and took a 3-point lead—and now *they* had a win expectancy of 95 percent. In the few remaining seconds, the Bills drove into position and kicked a field goal to tie. The game went into overtime, where the ball and win expectancy bounced back and forth until an intercepted Bills pass led to a winning Vikings field goal. A game as compelling as this reminded all of us fans both how great football can be and also how useless the win expectancy statistic is.

2022

The Vikings register the biggest comeback in NFL history in a game against the Colts. Down by thirty-three at the half, the Vikings fought back to take the game to overtime and win 39–36. The Vikings were playing at home and were the favorites, but if we stigmatized everybody who thinks they're a hero for doing what's expected of them at home, no one would ever take out the trash again.

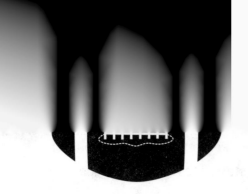

Fans

DAN The league only exists because of its fans, who pack into stadiums, gather around TVs, and buy any product with their team's logo on it, like Denver Broncos "Let's Drive!" spark plugs™! So, let's take a moment to celebrate some fans, like:

The Hogettes

These admirers of Washington's "Hogs" offense showed their allegiance by attending games wearing "old lady" dresses, hats, and plastic pig snouts. They looked ridiculous, yet also attractive to some lonely, rural viewers.

The Dawg Pound

The Browns' 1985 defensive line decided the opposing quarterback was a cat and they were dogs. Whenever they got a sack, they would bark and coaches would reward them by scratching the scruffs of their necks. The "Dawg Pound" became a rowdy part of the stands, with fans throwing dog treats at opposing teams and even bringing dog food into the stadium. This proved problematic for stadium vendors, as dog food tasted better than many concessions.

Packer Fans and the Lambeau Leap

If you haven't seen a Lambeau Leap, you haven't watched a game at Lambeau Field. Or the game you watched didn't have any Packer touchdowns and you were too lazy to watch a YouTube video of one. Or you started to watch a YouTube video and got annoyed at the ads and bailed.

Anyway, the leaping started in 1993 when LeRoy Butler ran a fumble back for a touchdown, jumped over the end zone wall in celebration, and gleefully landed in the throng of Packers fans. The Lambeau Leap was born. The *Milwaukee Journal Sentinel* later called this the forty-third greatest Wisconsin sports moment. (The forty-second greatest Wisconsin sports moment was when the Milwaukee Brewers discounted the cheese curds sold at games. Fans were overjoyed, then quickly constipated.)

These days, the Lambeau Leap is almost mandatory for all Packers touchdowns. Fans love it, but some players have noticed their wallets missing afterward. Police suspect a fan that always sits in the prime landing zone wearing several diamond rings and a cheese-hat made of solid gold.

Seattle's "Twelfth Man"

The Seahawks' famously loud home crowd refers to themselves as the team's "twelfth man." This "twelfth man" has been a big part of the Seahawks' success, yet because of them, Seattle is often penalized for "too many players."

Steelers Fans

The team has a rabid and loyal fan base, known for waving their "Terrible Towels." (The term originated in a review of a Pittsburgh-area Hilton.)

The Beauty of the Tailgate

ZACH POSNER AND DANIEL FURLONG

On weekdays, the asphalt surrounding an NFL football stadium is as vacant as Eli Manning's eyes as he tries to calculate a tip. But for a few hours before every home game, stadium parking lots transcend into magical football festivals where anything goes—a place where fat guys can shamelessly paint their bulging bellies bright blue, then go back to their desk jobs the next day and lead an HR meeting like nothing happened. An NFL tailgate is the only place besides church where not only is drinking alcohol at 9 AM on a Sunday encouraged, you might burn in Hell if you don't.

Tailgating is as American as apple pie, which, ironically, has no place at a tailgate since apple pie doesn't contain meat, cheese, or enough salt to take down an actual Chicago bear. The food at a tailgate is as eclectic as Cam Newton's hats. You've got grillers, smokers, pig roasters, giant turkey leg basters, Buffalo wing friers . . . The most important thing about tailgate food is that it should be consumable with one hand to free up the other hand for cooking more food, holding a beer, or shattering your new iPhone because your fantasy team's second-string running back is out with plantar fasciitis.

People who were late to their own weddings will arrive at the stadium five hours early so they don't miss a moment of pre-game pre-gaming. They aim to get drunk enough to let out years of repressed emotion and cheer their guts out, but not *so* drunk they forget they were at the game at all. (Unless you're a Browns, Jets, or Jon Gruden fan—then you might want to forget.)

The American football tailgate is the ultimate unifier. People from all races, backgrounds, and creeds can come together as one to scream profanities at a nice family from out of town who thought it'd be fun to check out an away game. *"Screw you for rooting for the team from the place you were born!"*

> **DAN** **Five Things to Never Bring to a Tailgate**
>
> - Kale, especially if you keep calling it a "superfood"
>
> - Different-sized forks ("one for fish, one for salad, one for the entrée . . .")
>
> - A still-baking soufflé you have to ask everyone to be quiet around so it "doesn't collapse"
>
> - A boombox for a quick pre-game Zumba dance workout
>
> - A book to read and a rented librarian that constantly shushes anyone making noise

From sea to shining sea, you can find all kinds of tailgaters: Cheeseheads outside Lambeau debating Favre versus Rodgers, Yinzers in Pittsburgh waving their Terrible Towels on the banks of the three rivers, a couple dudes in board shorts outside a Chargers game who got lost on their way to see the Dodgers.

Raiders fans used to be known for their out-of-control tailgates in Oakland, but since the Black Hole moved to Vegas, where they no longer have a parking lot, you might instead find a guy in Mad Max attire quietly taking in a Cirque du Soleil performance before kickoff.

The current kings of the tailgate are Buffalo Bills fans, who have become famous for hurling their drunken bodies through tables. But with the rising price of lumber and increased quality of plastics, who knows how long they can stay on top?

For as much as is known about tailgating, there's much that is still unknown. For instance, scientists have long attempted to figure out the "Tailgating Temperature Phenomenon," in which chugging a beer in a blizzard in Minnesota makes you warmer, but pounding that same beer in the sweltering Dallas heat cools you down. (Further testing is ongoing.)

Maybe the biggest tailgating mystery is why an out-of-shape father of two who hasn't played football since JV suddenly thinks he can run a post route at full speed between rows of cars and *not* pull a hammy. Yet each and every weekend, dozens of fans are seen limping into stadiums, wincing as they lower their butts into their seats. But they have huge smiles on their faces because they achieved the ultimate glory: catching a Nerf football in front of a crowd of drunken strangers.

2073

THE LEAGUE TODAY

DAN Today's NFL, renamed the "NFT" in 2027, is very different than it was fifty years ago.

There are teams all over the world, three on the moon, one on Mars, and one beneath the Atlantic Ocean, the only body of water that hasn't dried up. With unbridled expansion, there are now more NFL teams than Subway franchises, not surprising after putting "Chipotle Southwest" dressing on a sandwich was made illegal in 2053.

To its credit, the league has eradicated racism and all insensitivity. Instead of players' names, the backs of jerseys list their carbon footprint and favorite charities. Last year, the Spokane Garland District 87ers (the thirty-eighth spin-off from the 49ers) won the Super Bowl. They were led by quarterback Tom Brady, 96, who received a complete blood transfusion between every play. Postgame, Brady joked that those transfusions were the real MVP—"Most Valuable Plasma." This got a polite laugh from his team of doctors, who then stopped the interview so they could embalm the quarterback and load him back into the cryogenic chamber he lives in during the off-season, only coming out to annually retire and then unretire.

SEE YOU NEXT YEAR, FOOTBALL FANS!

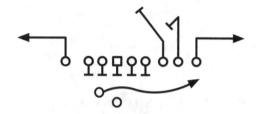

CONTRIBUTORS

Chuck Tatham (*Arrested Development, How I Met Your Mother, Modern Family*) splits his time between Los Angeles, New York, his native Canada, and any Vegas casino that hasn't banished him. An acclaimed high school football player who hung up his cleats in college to focus on sleeping and fermented beverages, Tatham lives and dies, but mostly dies, with his beloved Minnesota Vikings.

Christine Nangle (@nanglish) was born and raised in Philadelphia. She has written for several comedies including *Kroll Show, Inside Amy Schumer, Saturday Night Live,* and *The President Show,* and currently lives in Los Angeles where she writes for *The Simpsons.*

Andy Richter (@AndyRichter) is an actor and alleged comedian living in Burbank, California, with a large dog. He hosts a podcast called *The Three Questions.*

Donick Cary (donickcary.com) got his start writing for *Late Night with David Letterman.* He then moved to *The Simpsons,* where he won an Emmy. Cary has since written for and produced *New Girl*, *Silicon Valley*, *A.P. Bio*, *Bored to Death*, *Just Shoot Me!*, and *Parks and Recreation*. The year 2020 brought the release of Cary's feature directorial debut, *Have a Good Trip: Adventures in Psychedelics*, which was selected by SXSW and debuted on Netflix, remaining in the top five most streamed programs for over a month. Cary is a loving husband and father when he is not rooting for the Raiders, Celtics, Dodgers, and/or whatever the football team from Washington is currently called.

Zach Posner (@zachbythepound) and **Daniel Furlong** (@danielfurlong) have written for *The Simpsons*, the NFL Network, and the ESPYs. Posner is a Jets fan who once got out of a public intoxication ticket by spelling Laveranues Coles backward. Furlong is a Giants fan who loves the team so much that he hasn't watched them play football in five years.

Brian Kelley has written for *The Simpsons* for over twenty years, all of them with Joel Cohen, which has been hard. Before that, he led research and development at the famed Xerox PARC laboratories, where he invented the modern personal computer, object-oriented programming, and the laser printer. Joel Cohen didn't work there, which was probably why Brian Kelley was able to get so much done.

Broti Gupta (@brotigupta) is a comedy writer in Los Angeles, California. She does not know much about football. One time in gym class she made a touchdown during the football unit and the ball hit her mouth hard enough that her braces scraped up her gums. The kid who passed the ball to her cried. Seventh grade was hard.

Robert Cohen, the pride of the Canadian Rockies, has worked as a television writer/producer and director for more years than he cares to accept. His expansive writing career includes *The Ben Stiller Show* (for which he won an Emmy Award), *The Big Bang Theory*, and *Saturday Night Live*. His directing credits include *Black-ish*, *Maron*, *Lady Dynamite*, and *Somebody Somewhere*, as well as numerous commercials for national and international brands that have won multiple awards. His work has been praised by Michael Moore, Ridley Scott, and others, not including his parents.

Raber Analytics (@MatthewRaber11) was founded by Matthew Raber. They have provided analytics for several sports conferences and an unnamed National Hockey League team (hint: It's not the Nashville Predators).

Michael Price (@mikepriceinla) is a writer and producer on *The Simpsons*; he also co-created the Netflix animated comedy series *F Is for Family*, and wrote and produced a series of animated specials for LEGO Star Wars. This is his first published work of non-cartoon writing. He lives in Los Angeles with his wife, the real writer, Monica Holloway.

Illustrators

Brian Bowens (@bbsketch) has worked with many leagues, teams, brands, and players. He's also created huge custom canvas pieces, murals, illustrated comic and children's books, customized sneakers, and much more. He drew the images in this book, with the exceptions listed below.

Codey Dauch (@codeydraws) is an Ohio-based illustrator who loves his wife, his children, and, unfortunately, the Cleveland Browns. He drew all the helmets featured in this book.

RC Designs is a New York–based fashion designer and sketched the drawing of Guy-Louis DuPuy.

ACKNOWLEDGMENTS

The authors would very much like to thank all the talented people who helped birth this book. These literary midwives include all our contributors and illustrators, but also so many more.

A book full of occasional accuracies and inaccuracies is hard to both fact-check and fiction-check, and much of that burden fell on Jesse Wachtel and Meghan Kiely, who, if they complained, did it softly so we could ignore them. Impossible to ignore is the amazing and tireless work of our editors at BenBella, Leah Wilson and Alyn Wallace, and our copy editor, Elizabeth Degenhard. They even had to edit this section—they're like doctors doing surgery on themselves! While we're singing (writing) the praises of the people at BenBella, let's also give a shout-out to Sarah Avinger (for the cover) and the entire design team for turning a rambling format into something pleasing to the eye (if also annoying to the brain and wallet that paid for this book).

More thanks to book agent Jeff Silberman, uber-agent Paul B. Anderson, and all their associates for helping put all of these disparate pieces together as easily as if they were a jigsaw puzzle of "Hot Air Balloons of Belgium."

I guess we also need to thank our families or else there's gonna be some really silent, angry stares at breakfast, so thank you, families.

Lastly, has a book ever thanked the readers? Especially the ones that read the acknowledgments? Without finding out the answer to the question, thank *you*, reader. Your bravery and sacrifice will not be forgotten.

INDEX

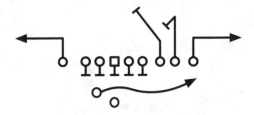

ABOUT THE AUTHORS

Known as "the best thing to come out of Cincinnati after Jerry Springer" and blessed with corn-fed good looks, **Dan Patrick** has been wafting into our eyes and ears for over four decades. An ESPN anchor for eighteen years, he's hosted *Football Night in America*, the Olympics, and now *The Dan Patrick Show*, heard on 400 radio stations across the U.S. and seen on Peacock some places. He was inducted into the Sportscasting Hall of Fame in 2020 and the Radio Hall of Fame in 2021.

Joel H. Cohen is a three-time Emmy winner and a writer/producer for *The Simpsons* (even though they'll deny it). He would be a Seahawks fan if he wasn't in so many fantasy football leagues that he's forced to root for every team and player to varying degrees (yes, this is a cry for help). He can be found on Instagram as @sportswrong.